The Crooked Path
A Journal of the Nameless Art

Contents

A Letter From the Editor	2
A Call to Writers & Authors We want to publish you!	3
Guided Visualisations through the Caucasus by Michael Berman	4
The Thinking Witch Top Reads of 2010 with Steven Posch	6
Lighting Old Paths with Illuminary Witches: An Interview with Janet Farrar and Gavin Bone by Tony Mierzwicki	9
Storm Mother by Veronica Cummer	18
Sonnets to The Morrigan by SP Hendrick	20
The Witch the Well and the Dark Rider: The Crossroads of Faery Practices, Old Religionist Witchcraft and Southern Conjure by Orion Foxwood	22
Pagan Parenting with Renee Berg	30
The Future Through the Writing on your Forehead by Michael Berman	33
Pendraig Publishing Catalogue Check out all the books available through Pendraig Publishing	37
Invocation and the Ancient Art of Ritual Possession by Peter Paddon	53
Gardner REDUX by Ann Finnin	61
The Crooked Paths Season Spotlight Winter Spotlight shines on Visceral Magick by Peter Paddon	67
Before the Battle by Peter Paddon	72

The Crooked Path Journal, Issue 7, Winter, January 2011

Edited by Peter Paddon

Cover Design & Interior Graphics / Typeset & Layout by Jo-Ann Byers-Mierzwicki

Published © 2010
by PENDRAIG Publishing
All Rights Reserved

ISBN 978-0-9827263-4-1
ISSN 1945-0621

The Crooked Path Journal is a quarterly magazine for Traditional Witches,
Cunningfolk and other practitioners of the Nameless Art.

The Crooked Path
A Journal of the Nameless Art

A Letter From the Editior

If I ever doubted it before, I now have hard proof that time is slipping by faster than ever. It has been over a year since the last issue of the Crooked Path Journal, and that just won't do. I offer my heart-felt apologies for this, but no excuses. Life got in the way for a while, the recession, my own crazed one-man-media-empire schedule did too, but none of that is anyone else's fault.

Despite all that, I've had the fortune of receiving a steady stream of supportive emails, asking when the next issue will be out. Well, here it is, and I hope you will agree, it has been worth the wait.

Our talented layout artist, Jo-Ann, has taken over the layout of the Journal as well as most of our books, and she's given the old bird a brand new look. In addition, we've managed, by sleight of hand, a small change in the physical dimensions, plus dark incantations in the small hours of the night, to give you a Journal that retains the quality, has more content, yet is actually cheaper. I hope you are as happy with that as I am.

The return of the Journal also marks the return of the podcast, and the imminent release of my new book, "Visceral Magick", which also suffered from the same delaying issues that this Journal did. I hope you will find that the wait was worth it for these as well.

Next month will see the arrival of PantheaCon, one of our favorite events, and I hope to get to meet new and old friends there, as well as present my workshop on "Invocation and the Ancient Art of Ritual Possession". There is a chance I will be attending a Druid event in the UK in July, and I will certainly be visiting North Carolina again for Shadow Harvest, and hopefully a few other places too.

Pendraig Publishing has been busy, even with the Journal and podcast on hiatus. We've published a book on Sybil Leek, and several books by Ray Buckland, including a reprint of the classic "Practical Color Magick", which will be on the shelves any day now.

So there you have it. I am really glad that the Journal and podcast are up and running again, and I'd love to know what you think - we've also revived the website, www.crookedpath.org, where there is a forum waiting to be filled with lore and discussion. I'd love to see your opinions of the Journal posted there.

Bendith,
Peter Paddon

The Crooked Path
A Journal of the Nameless Art

A Call To Writers and Authors

Have you have written a good article on a topic of interest to Traditional Crafters? Why not submit it to the Crooked Path Journal?

We are interested in anything relevant to non-Wiccan Witchcraft, Folk Magick, folklore etc., whether it is a single article, a series of articles, or a regular column.

We want to publish YOU

Please email your submissions to: Submissions@PendraigPublishing.com. In the Subject area please mark it as "Journal Submission".

If your article includes images please ensure that all images are royalty free 300 resolution files. We are able to accept most file types but tiffs are prefered. Please include a short bio to let the readers know about you.

What are you waiting for?

Email us at
Submissions@PendraigPublishing.com

The Crooked Path Journal

Guided Visualisations through the Caucasus

with Michael Berman

Spending any length of time in a region as ethnically diverse and conflict-ridden as the Caucasus means constantly having to walk a conversational tightrope. Everything from ordering a coffee (it may be called Turkuli – Turkish coffee - in Georgia, but in Yerevan you'd better say Armenian coffee) to place names (Karabakh's ancient city is Shushi to Armenians, Shusha to Azerbaijanis) is a potential minefield for the unwary traveller.

Learning to be diplomatic - often by just keeping your mouth shut - is the key to navigating Caucasus conversations. But it's not always easy. Armenians, Azerbaijanis and Georgians (not to mention Abkhaz, Ossetians, and the dozens of other peoples scattered around the region) are passionate about their histories and love a good argument.

One especially contentious topic is the subject of "firsts." As home to some of the world's oldest civilisations, the Caucasus is rife with arguments about who did what first - who were the first people to adopt Christianity, who were the first to invent a written alphabet, and who were the first to settle a particular patch of land. And the competition to claim firsts can lead to a lot of good-natured teasing.

There is a popular joke in Armenia, for example, about how Mesrop Mashtots, the inventor of the Armenian alphabet, had also invented the Georgian alphabet by throwing a leftover plate of spaghetti on the floor. The Georgians also have a joke they never tire of telling visitors to their country that makes fun of how Armenians always claim to have done everything first. It's about a team of Georgian archaeologists claiming to have discovered wires in an ancient site, proving that Georgians were the first to have telephone lines. The next day, so the joke goes, the Armenians discovered a site without wires and claimed to have had mobile phones instead. At other times, the debate over "firsts" can be deadly serious, like when discussing the territorial struggles - over Abkhazia, Nagorny Karabakh or South Ossetia.

What can be generally agreed on, though, is that the Caucasus is undoubtedly one of the cradles of civilization - the land with which the earliest folklore of Europe is connected, the land where Noah's Ark is said to have settled, and the land of the Argonauts and of Prometheus. It is also a region that has been called the geopolitical pivot about which everything sways - American economic interests, Russian American economic interests, Russian territorial interests, and Islamic religious interests. It is a place where mountains reach the sky, where continents meet, where empires used to intersect and where a multitude of languages mix. Additionally, it can be described as a place where unimaginable, unspoiled beauty and everyday barbarity can be found side by side. And all of these different aspects can be found reflected in the tales to be found in this collection.

Michael Berman BA, MPhil, PhD, works as a teacher and a writer. His publications include All God's Creatures Stories Old and New, Journeys Outside Time - Shamanic Ballads, Shamanic Stories and coming soon, Guided Visualisations through the Caucasus for Pendraig Publishing; The Power of Metaphor for Crown House. Michael has been involved in teaching and teacher training for over thirty years, has given presentations at Conferences in more than twenty countries, and hopes to have the opportunity to visit many more yet. Although Michael originally trained as a Core Shamanic Counsellor, these days his focus is more on the academic side of shamanism, with a particular interest in the folktales with shamanic themes told by and collected from the peoples of the Caucasus. For more information please visit www.Thestoryteller.org.uk

The Thinking Witch with Steven Posch
Top Reads of 2010

Looking over what I've read during the past year that in my opinion has something new to add to the conversation, I find that—no surprise here to anyone that knows me—the cream are all difficult books: both literary and academic.

Fiction first:

Alan Garner,
Thursbitch
(London: Vintage, 2004)
This is Alan Garner of Weirdstone of Brisingamen fame, all grown up, and has he ever got a tale to tell. If there had been an amanita-chewing, bull-worshipping Dionysiac cult still alive in 17th-century Cheshire (!), complete with songs, prayers, invocations, and proverbs, what would it have looked—and more importantly, sounded—like? Here it is, and he's such a word-wizard that he almost makes it work. He doesn't get everything right, of course, but he goes farther than anyone else. "There's nowt as He's not" (proverb). "O Bonny Bull, come thy ways" (invocation). This book is entirely about what English would have been like if it had been continuously spoken by our kind of people, filled with material you'll want to learn and use. Standard English, for example, doesn't distinguish between a place where three and four roads meet; "crossroads" can mean either. Witches' English, however—as one might expect—does distinguish between a "three-went" and a "four-went" respectively.

This is no easy read, Garner being a master of what's not said. Be ready to read between the lines. But it's richly worth the work: his words will sing in your head for days. All this so deeply rooted in the Cheshire landscape that it'll make your American heart break with envy. The name of a standing stone in a field near where Garner grew up was "the Bull Stang." I shit you not.

Allan Moore,
Voice of the Fire
(London: Indigo, 1997)
The British Songlines. Moore is the pagan James Michner (but can out-write Michner

any day of the year). A dozen pungent Guy Fawkes/Samhain tales set in Northampton and environs from (literally) 4000 BCE to the present. The clearest articulation of the role of the Man-in-Black/witchman that I've ever seen (he calls him the "Hob" or "Hobman.") Filled with November fires, severed heads, and giant black dogs. (He's got an explanation for the Templar Head that you will never—I promise—forget.) Another book so deeply immersed in local lore it'll make your teeth ache with envy.

This is yet another one with language as dense and rich as a Samhain fruitcake, studded with chewy nutmeats and piquant dried fruit. I hereby nominate "You're wrong like Hob's Hog" for "Craft proverb" status. (But you'll have to read the book to find out what it means.) The opening story is the hardest, written in what English might have sounded like if it had been spoken 6000 years ago. It's challenging, but persevere: force yourself to slow down and give the text time. Read aloud, if you need to. (It really does get easier, and the first story's the hardest.) This has been one of my favorite Samhain reads since it first came out, and every year I come away from it deepened and enriched

Now to non-fiction.

Emma Wilby,
Cunning Folk and Familiar Spirits: Shamanistic Visionary Traditions in Early Modern British Witchcraft and Magic
(Brighton: Sussex Academic Press, 2005)
The British academic press that published this one was entirely taken aback when it became a runaway bestseller, as actual practicing witches snapped up the meager first run. Wilby is a historian who in this book focuses on familiars, which she defines broadly as spirit-helpers in either animal or human form who aided the early modern British witch in her magic. This she compares to accounts of shamans from various cultures and their experiences with their own spirit-helpers. Naturally, she finds a lot of commonality between the two. Hmm.

If the God of Witches is preeminently Master of Animals (to me this seems patently obvious), it makes complete sense that he should offer guidance to his witches through their relationships with animals. Here's a how-to guide.

Stephen J. Yeates,
The Tribe of Witches: The Religion of the Dobunni and Hwicce
(Oxford: Oxbow Books, 2008)
This one gets my award for "Best Title of the Year." (Well, the first half, anyway.) Yeates is an archaeologist, and he believes that the West Midlands Anglo-Saxon kingdom of the Hwicce gave rise to the religion of the Wicce. This is impossible both linguistically and historically (since witchcraft did not become a religion until the 20th century, to trace its origins to a tribal religion of a thousand years ago is simply not credible). Yeates has clearly taken modern Wicca as a point of departure and is reading backwards, doing his damnedest to find a Triple Goddess paired with a God of Hunting—and better it be if

he's horned. Also, he doesn't write very well, and there's page upon page of information about which English creek flows into which English river, which in turn—in case you wondered—is a sub-tributary of the Severn.

So why should you read this book? For this reason: because, like Garner and Moore, Yeates climbs down into the landscape itself in search of his Hwicce-craft. The work that he does for the Severn/Cotswolds region is the kind of work that all of us need to be doing for our own areas, and Yeates can show us how to go about it.

First read this book, and then go down to the nearest river. I promise you, you'll see it with different eyes. Oh yeah: be sure to take an offering along.

David Lewis-Williams,
The Mind in the Cave
(London: Thames & Hudson, 2004)

Quite simply the best study I've ever read of how the human brain works and how it generates religious experience. The witch being one who thinks Third Thoughts—i.e. who watches herself think and thinks about her own thinking—this book is an indispensable guide to the varying states of consciousness, regular and altered. (Maybe that should be "altared" consciousness.) In language that even a non-neuro-physiologist like myself can (if not without some effort) follow.

This in itself would be worth the price of admission, but wait: there's more! Lewis-Williams applies the insights of brain physiology into reading the art of the Upper Palaeolithic caves of south-eastern Europe. (What, for instance, if the walls of the cave were thought of as semi-permeable membranes between This World and the Other?) This book will give you insights into how the ancestors may well have thought (and hence—third thoughts again—possible new directions in which to guide our own thinking) that, like most good ideas, will seem utterly obvious—once someone has gone to the work of articulating them. Another hard read that's more than worth the work.

OK, those are my picks for the *"Thinking Witch Top Reads of 2010."* **Next?**

Happy New Year,

Steve

Poet and storyteller Steven Posch, known as "the pagan rabbi" and the "Father of Paganistan," is one of the Twin Cities' preeminent Men-in-Black. He is keeper of the Minnesota Ooser.

The Crooked Path Journal

Lighting Old Paths with Illuminary Witches

Janet Farrar and Gavin Bone

Janet Farrar and Gavin Bone are prolific authors who have written many books on witchcraft. Janet is possibly best known for co-writing The Witches' Bible : The Complete Witches Handbook with her now deceased husband Stewart Farrar, while Gavin is remembered for co-writing a number of more recent texts with Janet. Background information is available at their website http://www.callaighe.com/

Janet and Gavin left their home country of Ireland and toured Australia from January to February 2001 presenting well received workshops and lectures. On 21 February 2001, Tony Mierzwicki had the privilege of interviewing Janet and Gavin. The interview was serialized into a number of portions with the intention of publishing them in a now defunct Australian magazine called Psychic Interactive. After the first two portions were published, the magazine folded. The Crooked Path Journal has decided that, because of its importance, the interview should be made available in its entirety, serialized into three installments, the first of which will contain the previously published portions, while the other two will contain the hitherto unpublished portions, and thus be exclusive to readers of The Crooked Path Journal.

In this installment, Janet and Gavin discuss how they got started in witchcraft, what witchcraft means to them, and they give insights into their own spiritual practices and the remnants of pagan magick in their Irish homeland. In the second installment, Janet and Gavin will discuss Gerald Gardner (the founder of Gardnerian witchcraft), Doreen Valiente, Alex Sanders (the founder of Alexandrian witchcraft), initiation and vital information for young people seeking to join a coven for the first time. In the third installment, Janet and Gavin's will discuss their vision of the future of witchcraft, provide essential book recommendations, and reveal their thoughts on Australia.

Janet: *Australia is a very new continent.* Witchcraft here is in its infancy. We are trying to develop the spiritual path of the witches of Australia by educating them in exactly not just the history of witchcraft, but also in practical workshops on how magick happens, how to use your natural energy, how to balance it, and how to take it forward to create what generally is termed magick. By the way, there is no such thing as magick. No, not at all. Same as there is no such thing as supernatural. Everything that we do is a perfectly natural development of human spirituality, and anybody with proper training can do it, absolutely anybody.

Tony: So how would you describe yourself and the spiritual path that you're on?

Janet: Technically I'm known in the movement as a wiccan. I don't like that word, I prefer to use the old word for it, a good hearty word, witch. I'm a witch.

Tony: What about you, Gavin? How would you describe yourself?

Gavin: I classify myself as a witch as well, like Janet. I also classify myself as a priest probably before anything else, in that I have a connection to deity. My role in life is to bring deity into the lives of other people, to bring spirit to them. So, I see that as part of my label I suppose you could say, although I try to avoid labels. But the way I work is very much in what you would call Shamanistic ways, the old ways of Northern Europe, which I bring into my way of working. But I see these just as tools for the eventual goal which I am trying to achieve.

Tony: OK, so you both describe yourself as witches. How would you define the term witch?

Janet: A witch is the remnants of an ancient priesthood, that goes back pre-Middle Ages, certainly well over 2000 years ago. It's the country wise man or country wise woman. It's a craft, the same as in any village you had the blacksmith, the tinker, the tailor, the candlestick maker, you had the village witch. And these were the people who directed the religious affairs of the village. And Gavin is quite right when he uses the term priest, it is a priesthood of pagans.

Tony: So Gavin, would you agree with that definition?

Gavin: Absolutely. I see wicca principally as a priesthood and a priestesshood. And we are trying to instill that back into the modern pagan movement, that this is what it should be about. Not just a priesthood for those in the pagan movement, but for everybody as a whole. What we find where we live in Ireland is we will have people turn up on our doorstep who are good Roman Catholics, who want questions answered. And Janet will do Tarot readings for them. They don't feel comfortable going to a Roman Catholic priest, so they come to us instead. And one of the things we've learned over the years is that when you look at all religions around the world, particularly the older ones – Hinduism, Shinto – there is very little difference between their practices and what we call Neo-paganism. There's just differences in culture, that's all. But again, the same goals are at work.

Tony: So what attracted you both to witchcraft? Can you tell us about some of your early experiences with witchcraft?

Janet: What attracted me to it was the opposite of what you might think. I was a Sunday school teacher, and I was a good Christian, and I went to save somebody, to get them away from what I thought was a terrible Satan worship cult. Instead, I found one of the most practical philosophies that I had ever come across in my life. Rather than going against the religion I had grown up with, it amplified it. I discovered that for the early years of being a witch I was very able to harmonise the Christianity that I'd grown up with, strip away the myths and legends from it, get back to its grass roots foundation, and then progress forward. And I realised that behind almost every monotheistic culture of the world there are pagan roots. In a sense I went back to the pagan roots that were there before Christianity.

Tony: What about you, Gavin?

Gavin: I started off looking for a way of boxing my spirituality, boxing my beliefs. I'd gone to the Christian church and it didn't make any logical sense what they were saying. They were saying it's this way. And I though that doesn't make sense, there can't be just one way. So I started to look for what I believed in, examining what I believed in and I discovered that I believed for instance in reincarnation. I thought, well, Buddhism believes in reincarnation, that makes sense. Then I started to look at the idea of polarity: male-female, black-white, good-evil, and I came across the ideas in Taoism so for a while, that made sense as well, that's Taoist. I got to Hinduism, a multi-god, polytheistic system, and I realised that those deities, those faces of the divine, represented images in culture, images in society and images in nature. I thought that makes sense as well. So for a while I used this sort of conglomeration of what I thought was instant culture, and then I picked up a book on wicca by woman called Doreen Valiente and realised that everything was in there but it was from a western cultural viewpoint. And that was a realisation, a discovery. I was a witch. One other fact which played a big part was at the time I was trying to avoid the fact that I was a healer. And I had always been drawn towards the psychic, towards the spiritual. The best label I found that I could describe myself in this society was a witch, a wiccan, which I continue to use to this day.

Janet: Witchcraft is very much a religion based on healing. It is the foremost and most important work that any witch does.

Gavin: If you look at the origins of magick, it starts with the shaman in the cave, going right back to the stone age, trying to drive out the evil spirit which is possessing somebody who is ill. So the first forms of magick were to do with healing. So for us it's a healing tradition. And that's something else we're trying to do at the moment, re-instill this original direction within wicca.

Tony: So have your lives been enhanced by your practice of wicca?

Janet: I've been practicing the craft, as it is known, since 1970, and the rewards that I have had from practicing this old philosophy have amplified my life a thousand fold. I wouldn't want it any different.

Gavin: I can't divorce my life from my spirituality, it's something they do in monotheistic religions. Going to a church on Sundays, and that's it, that's your spirituality. I can't do that. It is my life. My whole life is enhanced by it. To me it's very difficult to answer the question, because the two are so intertwined for me, they're indivisible.

Tony: What sort of spiritual practices do you practise on a regular basis? What sort of rituals do you perform?

Janet: There are personal private rituals and then there are the ones that involve all the members of our group. The private ritual always starts for me the moment I get up in the morning. The first thing I do is I take care of the needs of my deity, and my deity likes to be surrounded by fresh flowers, the scent of perfumes, incenses, oils. So every morning I make libations and offerings to that deity and right throughout the day I'm performing small rituals in one form or another to deity and that can be as simple as, something that the human race has lost quite sadly as we've moved into the 21st century: kindness, politeness and manners. They're all part of a ritual, and it's something that's sadly lacking in modern culture. As far as the other aspects of ritual go, when our group get together we celebrate 8 festivals, celebrations of the cycles of the northern hemisphere seasons of planting to harvest. We also celebrate personal rituals. For example, we have rituals for children, the equivalent of a Christian christening, we have marriage rites, and we have funeral rites, and these are all part of our lives.

Tony: You mentioned your personal deity before, who is she or he?

Janet: We see the creative principle of the universe as male and female, the Lord and the Lady. The female aspect to me has a Norse name which actually just means the Lady, and that's Freya. Interestingly enough, she's a cat goddess, and once you put your life in the hands of the deity, and you say to that deity I am your servant, your priestess, she makes sure that you actually do what she wants. In our case every damn stray cat for miles seems to get dumped on my doorstep. I'm not joking! And the other aspect, the male aspect, is her counterpart, Frey, and his name just means, the Lord. He's a harvest deity, a corn deity. Of course, I live in heart of the Irish countryside, so I need a harvest deity to fulfil my needs, because local farmers will come to me and ask when to plant. And if I don't come up with the goods, then I'm in real trouble!

Tony: What about you, Gavin? Are there any particular deities that you feel very close to?

Gavin: I work with Frey and Freya as well. Freya is my principal deity, has been for over 10 years now. And that was what I call my real initiation, was actually becoming a priest of her. The initiation didn't take place in a magick circle, it took place in the space of a year in my life, which turned my life upside down, because I made a dedication to her, as her priest. I can see from that point onwards how my life has changed, actually very much for the better. But I work with other deities as well as is necessary.

Janet: We all do that, we both do that. I think to explain to people who don't understand, because it's very confusing when they hear people mention the word "deities," rather than "deity." As I said, we see the creator as male and female. But all these deities of the world, from every culture of the world, are faces that we put on the divine. For a Hindu, it could be the Durga, who is their mother goddess figure. To the ancient Egyptians, you might find them worshipping a deity called Anubis, who had the head of a jackal. We personify a deity by giving it identity and faces, so they're just aspects of the divine, the ultimate divine.

Gavin: We work with a lot of deities as we feel we need to. I will work with Norse deities, Woden, Donar, the god Thor. We will also work with Hindu deities, particularly, one called Ganesha. Because he's in fact the most worshipped deity in the world, you'll find him in almost every continent, you'll find a shrine to Ganesha somewhere. If you go to Bombay, there's a shrine of him in every taxi, because he's the remover of obstacles. He's the elephant headed god, and of course, for the Indians, the elephant was used for removing obstacles from the road. This is the symbolism of the deity, the elephant. We will use him, because he's worshipped so much around the world. He's a very powerful god, so when we invoke him, things happen. A good example from a few years back: around the world there were reports coming in during the festival of Diwali, that Ganesha had actually been drinking milk from bottles. And we thought, that's interesting, that makes a change from the bleeding Madonnas that you get in the Catholic church. So we decided that we would try actually feeding milk to a little Ganesha statue in our house. And, lo and behold, the milk disappeared! It actually happened.

Janet: And not because that cats got it! [laughter] It's far too high up for the cats to reach!

Gavin: One thing you should realise is that the deity forms you come across, 50% of their make up is what we give them, the other 50% comes from the divine. So it's not a groveling relationship which you get in some patriarchal religions, it's a working relationship of I'll do this for you, if you do this for me, it's a partnership. So for us in our lives with our personal deities, that's very much a partnership in our lives. We can't divorce ourselves from day to day deity in our everyday lives. And when you do that we find that we work a myth of those deities in our everyday lives. Once you start to understand deity you find you can work with more of them. Though, some we won't work with because we just don't get on with them. A good example is the west African, the Orishas, who rather than what you'd call deity are a higher spirit form which we try to avoid working with because we don't have the mindset, the cultural mindset, to work with them, which is something we warn people about. We don't have a problem with Voudon, we understand where it comes from. But for some people it is very difficult to understand that if you give yourself over to a Voudon deity it takes your life over very completely and is very jealous. It's what has been fitted to that culture.

Tony: Jealous in what respect? With respect to other gods?

Gavin: Yes. Basically, you worship them and that's it. You can't have anybody else. So we say to people, particularly westerners, avoid them. But we will quite happily walk into a Hindu temple, and worship in a Hindu temple. And if you do that, particularly if there's an Indian community, you'll be surprised at how welcome you are, because to them, their religion is open to everybody.

Tony: Tell us about spiritual practices in Ireland, your home country.

Gavin: Well, Ireland's rather interesting, because during the height of the witch trials, less than 10 people were actually prosecuted for witchcraft...

Janet: Or executed...

Gavin: Or executed, for that matter.

Tony: Does that mean that not many people were practising witchcraft in Ireland?

Gavin: No, it's because the magickal traditions had been traditionally part of the Druidic past. Now Druidism in Ireland was part of a caste system, very similar to the feudal system which came later, where you had an upper class who were the educated intelligencia, and this is what the Druids were. So you couldn't be a king unless you were a Druid, you couldn't be nobility unless you were from a Druid family, and again it was in the family. So when Christianity came along in Ireland, what it did, is it did what it does everywhere - it pinpointed and targeted the people who were nobility and Christianised them first. Well at that time Christianity merged very happily in with paganism, so Druids quite happily became monks or priests, while continuing to practise the old pagan ways. It's one of the reasons the Ogham script developed in Ireland. The Ogham script is a fusion of a Latin vowel system with the old Druidic tree lore. It was a way of passing it down through Chrisitianity. So as time went on of course Christianity got a stronger foothold. The old deities were hidden behind the saints in Ireland, very similar to the African Santeria practices. So for instance, St Brigit was actually a Christianisation of the goddess Brigid. St Patrick took on many of the aspects of the god Lugh. So this carried on in Irish tradition and many of the aspects of magick took on Christian forms rather than neo-pagan forms. These are some of the things we've come across in Ireland. For instance you have holy wells all over Ireland. Their use dates back well before the coming of Christianity, in fact even before the coming of the Celtic peoples into Ireland. But there were magickal traditions associated with them. Leaving stuff at the wells, hanging stuff from the trees next to the well. And these are all pagan traditions which are carried on, but they carried on in the form of it being Irish Roman Catholicism. One of the most interesting finds we've come across is in an envelope in a tree. When we carefully opened it there was a prayer to St Martha and it was a threat. It said basically "Blessed St Martha please give me this, this, this in my life. If not I won't light candles to you in the Lady Chapel and I'll turn the statue of the Madonna upside down in the church." And this is an actual old form of spell work, which you come across in old forms of paganism. It's that working with deity

"I'll give you this, this and this if you do this for me, if not, well, basically I'll ignore you."

Janet: One of the loveliest ones I ever saw was really cheeky. It read "Holy Mary conceived without sin, help me to sin without conceiving."

Gavin: We have been asked on occasion to do some rather interesting things in Ireland because that magick is still there. We were asked to come down to a village. In this village there was one church and two pubs. In Ireland there's a general rule. There should be basically a pub per church in a village of that size. The two pubs were fighting it out. They were cursing each other, and we were asked by one pub to go down there and actually lift a curse. And somebody in the village was doing a curse called burying the sheaf. And it was a memory of the old corn king ritual, where at the end of the Lammas season, the end of Lughnasadh, August, you took corn, made it into a corn dolly and you buried it in the soil as a sacrifice for the coming year. But what was being done was this corn dolly was being made. It was being named as a person in the village and then being buried in the field with the Catholic Last Rites. It was actually a form of cursing. And we were at one stage going to actually lift the curse on that pub because it had been made against the publican. So you still have these little things go on in Ireland. So although the spirituality there is on the face of it Christian Roman Catholicism, when you start to go out into the countryside you find the remnants of paganism still there. The problem is that a lot of neo-pagans, modern pagans, go over and expect to see blatant paganism. They see the ancient sites, they see the stone circles, they see the burial mounds, places like New Grange, and they see places which appear to be Catholic worship. But they don't actually see what's behind it, what's actually really going on. And that's one of the things that we found from living there that the paganism there is still alive, the magick is still alive in the Christian culture there.

Never Previously Published! Don't miss the next installment of this great interview in The Crooked Path Journal Issue 8.

Tony Mierzwicki is the author of "Graeco-Egyptian Magick: Everyday Empowerment" and a forthcoming primer reconstructing Classical Greek religion. He has contributed to various anthologies and magazines. He has presented workshops recreating ancient magickal practices in the United States and the east coast of Australia since 2001, drawing on his practice of ceremonial magick which he began in 1990. Tony's wife, Jo-Ann has been co-facilitating his workshops since 2004. Tony completed three degrees at the University of Sydney - MA, BE and BSc. He is on the Board of Directors of Cherry Hill Seminary.

The Crooked Path
A Journal of the Nameless Art

NEED TO ADVERTISE YOUR STORE OR EVENT?
CHECK OUT OUR LOW RATES

Ad Size and Rates

Two page spread	13"wide x 7.50" high	$80.00
Full Page back cover (COLOR)	7.5" wide x 9.25" high	$60.00
Full page	5.75" wide x 7.50" high	$40.00
Half Page	5.75" wide x 3.75" high	$30.00
Quarter Page	2.875 wide x 1.875" high	$20.00

There is limited spacing for two page spreads and a full page back cover (color) We can put two half size ads on the outside back cover, but *only* if there is no full page ad.

Discounts

Get the Fifth one Free!
Prepay your ad to run in four consecutive issues and receive a fifth ad of the same value free!

File Types and Format

We are able to accept most graphic file types (TIF, GIF, PDF, PNG, JPG, and DOC. etc.) with a resolution of 300 dpi or higher. Display ads must be provided as digital files (via e-mail or on CD).

Send separate files of images in case scaling down doesn't work. Alternately, text and associated graphics may be submitted, but in this case, layout of the ad will be up to the Advertising Director and Editor.

Email artwork and any other relevant materials to: ads@pendraigpublishing.com. Please include the legal and business names of the advertisers and the issue in which you would prefer your materials to appear.

For complete details regarding our advertising terms and conditions
please visit:
www.PendraigPublishing.com
or contact us at:
ads@PendraigPublishing.com

The Crooked Path Journal

Storm

Flame and darkness
She rises up
Cloaked in raven feathers
In the tiny mirrors of the moon.
One day She shall be known by many names
Worshipped
Feared
Demeaned
Implored
The terrible Queen of the Crossroads
Of ghosts and wolves and witches,
She who knows the way below
The secrets of tree and grave.
To some She shall always be the perfect rose
The one that burns
In the garden of desire
And shall never succumb to death.
While Her green eyes burn
The light of a fallen emerald
And the tangles of Her hair move and drift
Serpents and cords and spider's silk
The currents of the winds
Worlds upon worlds.
Hear Her as she calls—

The Crooked Path Journal

MOTHER

The voice of the desert
That wraps the mountain in fire,
The voice that seduces the goat-gods
Who bear the mark
Of crooked lightning upon their brows.
She calls—
And the owl people come
Carrying Her own to the witches' heart of old
The deepest cave
Where light first fell and summoned clay to understanding,
There to receive the blood of renewal
His blood and Hers
And with it the memory of the beginnings
The knowing of the Elder Ones.
Crowned by thorns and peacock feathers
She is the throne
No king can resist
No kingdom deny
No heart refuse
For She is of old the Mother
Of storm and blood and madness
Of secrets and solitude
Of all that cannot be destroyed
So long as love remains.

Veronica Cummer a practicing witch for over 20 years and author of three books--Sorgitzak-Old Forest Craft and Masks of the Muse. To Fly By Night-The Craft of the Hedgewitch. In the past she was a writer and artist for Pagan Ink, a Twin Cities magazine. More recently, she has been published in newWitch, The Beltane Papers, and The Crooked Path Journal, as well as the anthologies, Talking About the Elephant and Datura.

Sonnets to

I

Beyond the cold north wind she waits.
    I call
Words beyond words…
    no place…no time…no sound
Until the thunder crashes,
    sund'ring all
With tongues of lightning
    forking all around
My Lady answers
    on the windy storm
In silences
    within the tempest's eye
And with Her raven wings
    She keeps me warm
And teaches
    my immortal soul to fly.
There is no fear
    within Her sweet embrace
However fierce
    Her battle-face might be
She shows another aspect
    in this place:
A patient teacher,
    guiding, guarding me.
How could I ever fear Her touch,
    Her kiss
When She has let me see Her once like this?

II

My Lady shows me battlefields of old
Bone-strewn, skull-strewn
    most ancient blood-soaked ground
So stark and lifeless,
    silent, deathly cold…
I feel no horror,
    but the peace they've found/
One skull looks up,
    its dead grin mocking me
And I recall the pleasure of the fight:

Adrenals pumping battle ecstasy…
She smiles and nods,
    no pity for the knight,
The warrior trained,
    whose passion was this field,
Who fought and died
    as he had wished to do
And to My Lady's kiss
    did finally yield
When sword-pierced heart
    at last had proven true
And She, in Queenly splendour
    led him home
Away from rotting flesh
    and bleaching bone.

The Crooked Path Journal

The Morrigan

III

I hear the eerie keening
    Bean-Sidhe wail
And listen closely
    to My Lady's voice
In song
    which reached through the Veil.
I do not weep in sorrow;
    I rejoice
To know someone,
    his lessons finally learned
For this brief life,
    upon this mortal plane
Has closed his eyes
    to take the rest he's earned
Until the next life
    brings him back again.
She stirs the Passion,
    be it Lust or Rage
Seducing us into both
    Life and Death,
Each one the merest turning
    of a page:
The pause between each heartbeat
    and each breath,
Oh glorious Morrigan
    I am free
And transformed by the love
    I have for Thee

S. P Hendrick is the author of a wonderful trilogy, the Glastonbury Chronicles, and also a marvelous vampire story set in Celtic Britain, Son of Air and Darkness available through Pendraig Publishing.

The Witch, the Well and the Dark Rider:

The Crossroads of Faery Practices, Old Religionist Witchcraft

and Southern Conjure

By Orion Foxwood

> "Stand I at the Crossroads, at the place between night and day:
> And with my Witches figure open I the Faery Way.
> And, stand I at the crossroads at the place between life and death,
> and enchanted be this magic place with my Witch's breath."

Though there is often heated debate about the content and origins of the magical lore, customs and practices commonly referred to as "Witchcraft" in America, there is one thing witches agree on regardless of tradition or system; "that the Craft Arcane works with magic, the secret ways of nature and the relationship between humanity and the other worlds (seen and unseen) and the inhabitants of those worlds. This article is a brief discussion of my position on the folk ways of the Craft as seen through my eyes as a Traditional Witch, Faery Seer and Southern/Appalachian Conjure-man. By the way, it is time for the wise ones to stop warring and seek wisdom instead of rightness. We must live in "nobility of mind and purpose", but not in righteous resentments that binds the wild-force of the witch on the altar of mediocrity.

The ideas in this article are not definitive or absolute. But then, neither is the writer. Though we may have concrete guiding principles, neither I - nor you - are finished products. And, sad is the day that we close our minds and spirits to the in-flowing tide of love, wisdom and power that is present always, in all levels and in all forms. Rather, the ideas presented in this article reflect my understanding based on over 25 years of training, academic research and contemporary practice fused to a foundation of the cultural magic that I was born into and raised in the Shenandoah Valley of Virginia. They are for reflection and contemplation as the reader navigates their way through the gray roads of old world and old style folk witchcraft, conjure and cunning ways. For clarity- witchery, cunning, conjure and turning refers to similar practices in the traditions I work from. I have searched the dark forests of my inner being – and continue to do so - for the shadow-shapers and the wisdom keepers that taunt and teach. The practices in the streams of magic I discuss form the potency of the magic worker, but only after they have shape-shifted from humans of compliance to humans of congruence.

Most of humanity places highest value on their ability to function in the "negotiated general-population" agreements on our "shape" as dictated by basic roles, relationships and responsibilities. Though these elements have important value in our inter-social world of industry, function and performance; they lack the essential guidance in the "art of becoming". In this art, we (the seekers) "seek the star within the stone", which is that deep inner directive that willed us into birth. However, we were born to escape our soul cages and create ourselves in congruence with an ancient directive within. We were born to redeem the blood paradoxes of our ancestors and bring humanity into attunement, alignment and agreement with what I call "the original instructions". No one can give that directive, it must be discovered... summoned forth and conjured into the world. This level of congruence requires the seeker to meet the "Dark Rider" (the mercurial spirit of the crossroads in my conjure tradition), open the ancient well of memory where space is speaking in all things (the Faery well and Witch's cauldron or coracle), descend into voices of our blood (the river of blood with banks of sorrow and song), through the threads of illusion (encounter with she who is the Weaver also known as Old Fate) to the witch-flame of our awareness beyond the flesh-robes of form (the gate of awakening and the guidance of the Faery Children of the Dawn) to the driving beat of power that at the core of selfhood...the sun at midnight also known as the Witch flame, Conjure Fire, Faery Fire, Blue Flame, Child of Promise or Dreamer in the Land.

This process is written into the oral lore, practices, and witchery of all three of the primary traditions and systems I teach. Join with me, for a few pages, on a journey into the foundations, lore and "dreamscape" of my lineage and systems of witchcraft, seership and conjure. My hope is that it will fan the fires of enquiry and divine discontent within you and strengthen your resolve to lift the spelle of forgetfulness from yourself and release the potent forces of magic and abiding mystery. But, I advise, do your inner work. Know what your shadow- shapers and shape-holders are and clean out those ghosts that live in corners of your inner being. We were all born to become manifest magic when the tumblers of our lock come together in the combination of codes called: a) necessity; b) opportunity; and c) resource. We have a saying in my Craft tradition as follows "I touch you and your blood remembers"

The Roots of My Ways

Everything about how I view magic and spirit(ual) practices is formed on the foundations of my familial and cultural based roots. For clarity, when I say "spiritual", I do not simply mean a set of practices and beliefs centered on a desire to have a relationship with divinity grounded in moral guidance and preparation for the death. Rather, I mean the development of human awareness as a "spirit in a human expression". By this, I mean the development of full awareness of the illusion of individuation and the interaction between the appearance of separateness (the emerging human wave) and the unity of spirit (the ocean which issues and gives context to the wave). In my view and those of my culture, a spiritual person is one who knows and lives in accord with the ways of spirit and spirit beings (incarnate discarnate and non-carnate). Magic, as a philosophy and a way of life, is an active relationship with the creative, destructive and regenerative powers of the spirit world in all its guises. I am firmly convinced that all spiritual traditions, be they mystical, religious and/or magical existing to answer three guiding enquiries which I call "the sacred questions":

1) Who am I?

Who am I, as the seeker of truth and the hidden secrets of creation, an extension of the creation (an individualized package), a member of a species called "human" with a role, and who am I and my species in the context of the dream/ vision of this plane (on its Gaia surface and in its Luciferian fiery core).

2) What is it?

How did the universe (inner and outer) and our planet and her creatures (seen and unseen) comes into and out of being and "who" or "what" created them/us?

3) What is my role in it?

Since I am the only me their has ever been and ever will be, my creation was intentional. What was that intention and how can I attune, align and bring my inner and outer life into agreement with it?

And for the magic worker, there is one more:

4) How do I get interactively involved in the workings of it to produce a better human and spirit life for myself and others?

Magic, in its many forms involves an understanding of the rhythm (patterns, potencies and powers) and resonance (language) as understood from a direct interaction between the magic worker, the attending spirits at all level of life, and refined states of awareness that "press the coal of your being into the diamond of your becoming". For this step of development, the seeker should always remember that "the toucher is touched". This is an old saying to be mindful of the forces you conjure lest they shape you into the pain you have forgotten. This is why a true adept of these arts is ever diligent in understanding the heights and depths of their being. In this way the witch calls the right level of magical electricity into sound wiring. Otherwise, one could encounter an inner house-fire that rampages outward.

My family and the people I grew up with would have rarely used the words "Faery" or "Magic". Sometimes they would refer to the "Little People" or other more localized terms like "Woods Folk", "Water Men", "Green People" and other terms. Occasionally someone would say "Faery" but that was usually someone who read about them in books or who descended from Irish heritage more recent in immigration to America than those who had been in the Valley for more that 2-300 years. However, the "veil" was always intimately connected to three types of tokens: 1) signatures that would come to the seer such as a knock at a door, which would then be opened and a vision would appear; 2) "dreaming true" or simply having foreknowledge of events, which my mother called "the knowing"; or 3) direct communication from ancestral and other types (usually nature ones) of spirit beings that would bring messages. My mother had the #1 and #2 types of tokens, while I have #2 and #3. Because of this type of "blessing", I have always been able to be a "bridge for the spirits". There was a significant amount of lore about approaching the ancestral and nature spirits in the family, shared with my mother by Ms. Granny and given to me in informal chats etc and other social settings by elders in the community. "Faery Tradition" as I understand it in a cultural context is not a body of tightly woven material, but rather stories, parables, practical techniques and suggestions for avoiding these beings, placating them or gaining their favor. I always had a particular affinity with the unseen company. In fact, many elders in the community said to me that I had an uncanny way with the spirits…one which they either rarely seen or never saw in their lifetimes. Occasionally, someone would simply clutch their children and cover their eyes when me or my mother walked by.

In reflection, there are core elements that my cultural tradition(s) share in common with the Craft line I was initiated into later in life and the Faery Seership practices I developed in partnership with my Faery wife, ancestral spirits and the guidance of the blood, bone and star rhythms my veil allows me to perceive. Though inspired by elements of traditional Faery practices and lore, the Faery Seership I teach is a combination of research, oral lore, inspired material and contemporary practices. The Craft tradition I practice is the combined wisdom of all my teachers with specific and primary focus on the oral teachings of my Witch Mother, Lady Circe. She was a 5th generation hereditary witch who lived in Toledo Ohio. I am one of three people honored to carry her mantle. The conjure material I teach comes from my blood elders and traditional conjurers in both Appalachian (Virginia and West Virginia) and Southern (Virginia and New Orleans) traditions. All three of these streams of magical practice have potent spirit beings, magical forces and wisdom teachings that are much needed in our changing world. Below I have listed some core concepts and practices that span these three traditions.

Core beliefs and Practices

- Blood mysteries: Each of us descend through the rhythm of time from those before us. We may be described as a surfacing stream from the river of blood. This folkloric image describes a flow of ancestral presence that moves into and through us. The ancestral spirits are the one inner order that we all are being initiated into with each step we take, each breath exhalation and each moment we summon and each life-force investment and interaction we make.

Therefore, interaction with ancestral spirits (human and other) is constant.

- **The summoning:** all three of these systems incorporate lore and techniques for contacting and directing flows of energy and essence with a desired affect. We call this conjuring, witchery or enchantment.

- **The Void as cauldron, flame, crossroads, well or flame-** all three have a visionary images or techniques for mind-touching human awareness to the essential source-material manifestation and de-manifestation point or intelligence where magic/creation begins and ends. This point or state is the meeting point between human and the universal inter-sessory spirit that links the two whether that is the point where star and void meet, human and crossroads spirit meet (the Dark Rider), fire of enquiry with stellar being through the archway of flame.

- **Co-creation through force-form-flow techniques and spirit encounter and exchange** – Lore and techniques for "intra-terrestrial" states of being and intelligences (spirits) for the cross-consciousness form boundary work which invites a type of human-other, human-planetary and universal unified state of life.

- **An animated worldview wherein life and intelligent states of life exist in all things, at all times, in all places and in all ways.** Or, as my momma always said "they is haints around every corner" and "ya neva know where the angels be".

- **The Value of these in our changing world-** So many seekers of the magic paths want control over their lives or at least that is what they think initially. In fact, they seek to belong...to be Sacred, to have the conscious ability to affect change in their lives (power) and to heal the illusion of aloneness.

- **The edge walker or crossroads spirit-** there is a being or stet of being that lives at the edge of human awareness and can bridge humanity back to a familial bond with the incarnate, discarnate and non-carnate spirit world. In my culture of conjure it is the "Dark Rider" at the crossroads or "Daddy Death" in the graveyard. In Faery practices it is the Co-walker. In the Craft it is the Horned Master whose stands at the boundary between human and other and parts his two horns of past and future to that in-between place where magic is made.

Well, there ya go! Herein are the thoughts of a Witch, Seer and Conjurer who has "divorced madness and married miraculous". I conjure good insight and magic that all who seek find the star of their yearning.

A Charm for the Reader-

*"Holy Flame,
holy Fire,
grant to you, your heart's desire.
Holy Fire,
holy flame,
grant it in the Old One's name.*

About Orion Foxwood

Orion was born in 1963 with the second sight in the Shenandoah Valley in Virginia, an area rife with the folk practices of the southern and Appalachian tradition. His mother, sister and himself were all born with what is known in his culture as "the veil"; a placental sheath over the eyes that denotes the "blessings" (another cultural term for sprit sight or second sight). Throughout his early life he was constantly exposed to faith healers, root-doctors, two-headed preachers (ministers who were also conjurers) and a host of spirit beings that forms the subtle landscape of his home place. These experiences and exposures formed the foundations of his spirit and spiritual worlds.

In his early twenties he was initiated into traditional old religionist practices (also known as traditional witchcraft or "the Craft"). He is a an Elder in Traditional Craft, High Priest in Alexandrian Wicca and primary teacher of the Faery Seership tradition as it is taught and practiced within the House of Brigh. He is also the founding Elder of Foxwood Temple and a primary founder of the Alliance of the Old Religion, a national network of covens in his line that have united to preserve the ways of his Elders. He was the co-director of Moonridge, a center for metaphysical, Craft and Faery studies in Maryland. Orion has over 25 years as a public health specialist and a clinician and holds a Masters Degree in Human Services.

For over 25 years, he has lectured in the United States and more recently in the United Kingdom on the Craft, Faery Seership and Southern Folk Magic and conjure practices. He is the author of The Faery Teachings (RJ Stewart Books, 2007), a collaborative CD project with RJ Stewart named Faery Seership, his newly released book The Tree of Enchantment (Weiser books, 2008), a four DVD set entitled An Introduction to Faery Seership (Pendraig Publications, 2010), and a collaborative DVD project with Katie Lydon Olivares (Pendraig Publications, 2010).

The Crooked Path Journal

Pagan Parenting with Renee Berg

Parenting is a vast topic that cannot be covered in a single class, book, and certainly not a single article. Being a pagan parent in some ways makes parenting easier, since many pagans strive to be in tune with the natural world. However, the challenge is may not be directly associated with what to do with your kids, so much as it may be functioning as a parent with integrity in a non pagan culture.

Traditional society often holds misconceptions about paganism that stem from ignorance and the portrayal of the pagan approach as evil by other religions and the media. The community in which one is raising their family will definitely have an impact on how "out" a pagan family might choose to be. This is unfortunate because, as Emerson said, *"Your actions speak so loudly, I cannot hear your words."* If we express our spirituality cautiously, we teach our children that there is a reason to do so. Younger children might read into parental caution that there is something inherently "wrong" or "bad" with pagan spirituality. Raising our children with pagan values, and concurrently teaching them to be selective in how they share these values is oxymoronic. And, unfortunately, sometimes necessary.

> *"You do not own your children; they are on loan to you from the future."*
> *Traditional Chinese Proverb*

The risks of raising children as "out" pagans are many. Depending upon the community in which a family lives, parents may face the scrutiny of school officials and child and family services.

So what is a parent to do? If a parent chooses paganism, and raises the children in that environment, the parent needs to be ultra responsible. So long as the children are healthy, well cared for, get to school on time and are prepared for class, as well as the home environment being reasonably clean, it is less likely to draw unwanted attention. Even my family has nosy neighbors in my liberal Los Angeles community. The home and yard are clean. The kids are friendly and courteous. When we have gatherings, the noise stops around 10 pm. We smile and say, "Hello", to our neighbors when we see them. I also hang mirror balls in front of my house, to reflect any negativity. Just in case.

Our kids are healthy. They have received all their immunizations. They attend school regularly. Their clothes are clean. They are clean. Sometimes they wear colorful clothing, but nothing different from what the average Valley teen might wear to school. A former principal called me to ask, "Do you know what your daughter is wearing? She looks like a slut." I replied, "Is she naked? No? Well I am glad she is testing your boundaries and not mine, since that is what teens do". It was amazing; the principal never pestered me, or my daughter again. I did not let the administrator drag me into a pointless dialog. Although I would not call this woman a friend, I can feel comfortable describing our interactions as cordial on the occasions we meet.

Conservative communities often focus on managing the lives of others. The best way to avoid that attention is, to the best of one's values, color inside societies lines. That is not to recommend abandoning fundamental pagan values, but to play by society's rules in other areas.

I am a strong advocate for public schools. When children attend a public school, they are working with teachers who have gone through a regimen equivalent to a master's degree to acquire their teaching license. Public schools are inherently diverse. Even though there may be challenges for pagan children, attending public school will teach them how to interact with myriad types of people. The more tools for living in a diverse world we can give our children, the more skilled they will be at creating a satisfying life for themselves. All parents get to do is provide experiences such that their children can create a life the children want for themselves. Insulating or isolating our children does not serve them in the bigger picture.

Be an informed consumer. Many school districts offer a variety of school types. Check to see if the local district has "alternative" schools, which are generally more open to diversity. It is important that pagan parents be informed about the curriculum offered within the district, and even the curriculum of the particular school you select. If the school is generally acceptable, but teaches a narrower view of a subject than you prefer, enrich your child's exposure with content you feel is important.

Once your children are in a school, be proactive. Volunteering for the school is one way to build acceptance for your children, and for you. Over the years, I have gone into schools as a "Rolling Reader", taught art, yoga, dance, and even crocheting! People are less frightened of that (or those) with whom they are familiar. Show up for school events when you can, join the parents' organization, participate in bake sales. Ask the teacher if s/he needs help. Share your talents. Are you good with gardening? How about cooking? Maybe you can teach music. The point is that by your presence, you will be integrated into the community, then, should something come up, you are part of the community already. Being part of the community can diminish the intensity of reactions.

Home schooling children isolates them. In our contemporary culture being pagan puts a family on the fringe of society as it is. There is magic in having the ability to interface with others. That being said, some parents will choose home schooling. Home schooling requires quite a lot of structure and discipline on the part of the parents and the children. My husband and I are both licensed teachers. There is no way I would take on home schooling my children. My job is to be a mother, to teach deep core values, to model having a healthy marriage, and to be the keeper of the nest. I model what it is to honor the Goddess in my being.

Even if you are home schooling, your local district can offer PE, and enrichment courses, such as music and dance. It may be possible to find others in the pagan community who also are choosing to home school. It is entirely reasonable to ask other adults working with your children for a live scan, even if you have circled with them innumerable times. You want to be sure that you are protecting your children from predators, who are inherently opportunistic.

If you home school, you can include all kinds of enriching curricular activities into your child's education. Teaching math and science through recycling, caring for animals, and gardening will make it much more fun, and real.

One of the glaring gaps in California's public curriculum is the absence of vocational education. A parent who home schools can teach geometry through carpentry activities or sewing. Cooking involves language, math, science, and even culture, depending upon the food being prepared. Teach children to look at the stars and identify to planets and constellations. Children can learn to make herbal incense. Drumming teaches patterning and music. Dancing is great exercise and, in the right context, can bring forth some very high level energies. As a life long meditator, I recommend teaching your children to quiet and focus their minds. Meditation as a practice can build their powers of intention as well as finding internal peace. Of course, another advantage is that home schooling allows parents to share important spiritual practices.

In point of fact, pagan parents sending their children to public school can offer their children those suggested enrichments.

Most hereditary pagans/witches I have met are proud of their lineage as adults. It may take some time for children to grow into that. When children are moving through Erikson's developmental stage of industry versus inferiority, and Piaget's cognitive stage of concrete operations, which is ages 6 to 11 years, children want to "fit in". This is normal and healthy for them. As pagan parents, do not embarrass them. Without abandoning your identity, try to be yourself in the context of their perceptions, with respect for their experience. So, when you go into the school for one reason or another, be mindful that the school is where your kid lives for 1080 hours a year. Be cool. Honor your children. How you treat your children has an impact upon who they will become. These spirits have come through you to this earth. For a very short while you have been charged with their stewardship. Your great work pays it forward throughout generations.

> **Once your children are in a school, be proactive.**

So Mote It Be.

Renee Berg holds a BA in Early Childhood Education, a Master's in Human Development, a multi-subject teaching credential, a single subject credential in dance, & a SAG card. She has taught grades pre-kindergarden to seniors. For the last 11 years Renee has been teaching at the college & university level. She is the author of the book, Practical Kindergarten. As a young woman, she danced for numerous rock bands professionally as well as having worked on a couple of films. Currently Renee hosts sabbats for solitaries & pagan oriented workshops in her home, The Winnetka Tower.

*A*rmenians even today believe there is writing on a person's forehead which tells his or her future and that this future is pre-determined. The person believed to be responsible for keeping a record of this information is Tir, the scribe of the supreme god Aramazd. (Aramazd was regarded as the father of all gods and goddesses, the creator of heaven and earth. The first two letters in his name, "AR" is the Indo-European root for sun, light, and life, and Aramazd was the source of earth's fertility, making it fruitful and bountiful). Through a meeting with Tir the scribe, you have the opportunity to find out what the future holds for you and to change it for the better.

The Future Through the Writing on Your Forehead

The wife of a farmer was taking care of the sheep in the fields when she gave birth to a child. A shepherd nearby saw an angel descend from heaven and write something on the baby's forehead. But since the shepherd could not see what was written, he asked the angel, "What did you do to that child?"

"I wrote his future on his forehead," the angel said.

"Why? Is he such an unusual child?"

"All human beings have their future written on their foreheads when they are born," the angel said, preparing to leave. "This child will fall from a tree and die at the age of seven."

The shepherd was very much interested: "I'll ask that woman's name, and after seven years, I will return to see if the angel's prediction comes true." And this he did.

After seven years he decided to find the woman and see how the child was. He found her house but saw that there was a large crowd gathered around it. "What has happened?" he asked a neighbor.

"The little boy who live here fell from a tree and died, and the parents want to kill the other boy who was playing with him. They say that because their son died, his playmate must die, too. Of course the playmate's parents won't permit this, and so the two families are quarreling."

"Oh, oh! The angel was right," the man said to himself, "but one death is enough. I must try to stop the second." He pushed through the crowd, went inside the house and asked the family about the trouble.

The first woman said, "My son was playing in the tree with this woman's son, and my boy fell off the tree and died. This woman's son should die, too."

"If your son fell off, why should my son die?" the second woman asked.

"Listen to me for a minute," the shepherd said. "Do you remember me?" he asked the first woman. "I am the shepherd you saw on the day your son was born in the fields. That same day, at the same time your son was born, an angel came down from heaven and wrote on his forehead. I asked the angel what he had writeen, and I was told that the little boy would fall from a tree at the age of seven and die. Now it has happened, and no one is to blame. Come, spare this little boy's life."

The first woman, seeing the truth of the argument, stopped asking for the life of the little boy. "What God has determined, we cannot prevent," she said.

What follows is a guided visualisation based on the story presented above. If you are working on your own, it is suggested that you record the script, perhaps with some appropriate background music. You can then lie somewhere comfortable, where you will not be disturbed, and play the recording back to yourself as you go through the process described.

The Mirror That Shows Your Future

SCRIPT FOR THE GUIDE:
(To be read in a gentle trance-inducing voice).

Make yourself comfortable and close your eyes. Take a few deep breaths to help you relax. Feel the tension disappear stage by stage from the top of your head to the tips of your toes. Let your surroundings fade away as you gradually sink backwards through time and actuality and pass through the gateway of this reality into the dreamtime. (When the participants are fully relaxed, begin the next stage).

Today's a very special day for you because you're being given an opportunity to see your future and, more importantly, to make changes now to ensure you have the best possible chance of turning it into what you want it to be.

Ahead of you what appears to be some kind of temple. Up three stone steps you make your way to an arched oak-panelled doorway. The doors are wide open for you, and within a deep blue carpet runs down the central aisle. At the end of it an indistinct figure swaying a censer perfumed with frankincense to and fro, enveloped by smoke. Breathe it in and feel centred. The smoke obscures your vision, but only temporarily, for as it clears the figure becomes clear to you – Tir the scribe and the keeper of the records. He stands by a full-length mirror. Notice both its distinct frame and shape. It shape seems to be that of a human body, your body in fact.

Tir motions to you to approach and join him, where he invites you to stand in front of the mirror and to look into it, in particular to see what is written on your forehead. And you have a minute of clock time, equal to all the time you need for this.

You're probably now wondering what you can do to change what you see. What you can do is work towards making a better future for yourself and those you interact with by learning from the mistakes you've made and by making sure you don't repeat them again. The time has come now for Tir to speak. And you have a minute of clock time, equal to all the time you need, to hear what advice he has to give you on this subject ...

You can make those changes that you really wish to make, for your unconscious mind is listening and will receive and act upon the messages it hears. And you will find, as this is happening, that you become much happier, within yourself - delighted with who you are, what you have and everything you can offer. What matters now, is that you take what you have learnt back with you and that you hold on to it. The time has come to give thanks for what you have received and to take your leave, to make your way back, down the carpeted central aisle of the temple, through the arched wooden doors, down the three steps and back to the place where you started from, where your new life awaits you.

Take a deep breath, let it all out slowly, open your eyes, and smile at the first person you see. Stretch your arms, stretch your legs, stamp your feet on the ground, and make sure you're really back, back in (name of the location), back where you started from. Welcome home!

Now take a few minutes in silence to make some notes on the experiences you had on your journeys, which you can then share with the rest of the group.

Or

Now take a few minutes in silence to make some notes on the experiences you had on your journeys, which you can then make a note of in your dream journal.

Or

And now you might like to turn to the person sitting next to you and share some of the experiences you had on your journeys.

Michael Berman BA, MPhil, PhD, works as a teacher and a writer. Publications include All God's Creatures Stories Old and New, Journeys Outside Time - Shamanic Ballads, Shamanic Stories and coming soon, Guided Visualisations through the Caucasus for Pendraig Publishing; A Multiple Intelligences Road to an ELT Classroom and The Power of Metaphor for Crown House, and The Nature of Shamanism and the Shamanic Story for Cambridge Scholars Publishing. Michael has been involved in teaching and teacher training for over thirty years, has given presentations at Conferences in more than twenty countries, and hopes to have the opportunity to visit many more yet. Although Michael originally trained as a Core Shamanic Counsellor with, these days his focus is more on the academic side of shamanism, with a particular interest in the folktales with shamanic themes told by and collected from the peoples of the Caucasus. For more information please visit www.Thestoryteller.org.uk

Books of Witchcraft

A Grimoire for Modern Cunningfolk — $10.95
A Practical Guide to Witchcraft on the Crooked Path — 978-0-9843302-1-8
Peter Paddon

A practical manual of Traditional non-Wiccan Witchcraft. The Crooked Path is a way of Crafting based on experiencing the Mysteries of Ancestors and the Sacred Landscape first-hand, and Peter guides the seeker through the basics with competence and humor.

Kindle Edition — $4.99 — 978-0-9843302-1-8
Limited Edition Hardcover — $75.95 — 978-0-9843302-2-5

A limited hardcover edition of 100 numbered and signed copies. This book includes the full text of the standard edition, a DVD of the author demonstrating some of the practical techniques, and an extra chapter on body fluids and sex magic. STILL A FEW COPIES LEFT

Balkan Traditional Witchcraft — $15.95
Radomir Ristic — 978-0-9796168-5-3

Published in English for the first time, this groundbreaking book by Radomir Ristic is a compilation of historical data, anthropological studies, and the authors own experiences and interviews with the Witches of the Balkans. Covering both theory and practice, the book gives a complete system of Balkan Traditional Witchcraft. English translation by Michael C. Carter, Jr.

Buckland's Domino Divination — $8.95
Fortune-Telling with Dominoes — 978-0-9827263-1-0
Raymond Buckland

Although today familiar to most people only as a game, dominoes were originally used by the Chinese for divination and fortune-telling. The reading of dominoes comes under the heading of sortilege and, as such, can be traced back to early Greek and Roman methods of divining the future.

Buckland's Practical Color Magick — $9.95
Raymond Buckland — 978-0-9827263-9-6

Color surrounds us in our world and this book can show you how to put that color to work. Color Magick is powerful, yet safe. It is creative and fun to do. It is the use of a natural element in a practical way. Color Magick can be used in meditation, healing, ESP, Tarot, crystal-gazing, ritual, candle-magick, and many other forms of magical practice. Learn all of its secrets in this exciting book!

**The Kindle version can be read on the Amazon Kindle reader or the Kindle app for iPhone

Books of Witchcraft

Hedge-Rider: $13.95
Witches and the Underworld   978-0-9796168-7-7
Eric De Vries

Hedgerider: Witches and the Underworld is a re-interpretation of (Hedge-)Witchery. Drawing from an extensive historical, folkloric and mythological body it re-attributes and re-defines Witchery as a Heathen Cult centred around the journey to the Underworld and contact with the Unseen.

Masks of the Muse $17.95
Building a relationship with the Goddess of the West   978-0-9820318-3-4
Veronica Cummer

By the poetry, prayer, invocation, and ritual contained within we can come to know the Muse and so know ourselves and the gifts we all have within us that demand recognition and expression. The path of the Muse may not always be an easy or a safe one, but anything worth having is worth paying the price for. Who is the Muse? Who are we?

Sorgitzak: Old Forest Craft $18.95
Stories and messages from the gods of Old Europe   978-0-9796168-6-0
Veronica Cummer

This is a book about the religion once practiced ages ago in the Old Forest region of Europe. The book contains channeled messages from the Gods of the Old Forest and from the fey, as well as stories, myths, legends, and bits and pieces of the old witch language.

Kindle Edition $4.99   978-0979616860

Sybil Leek: Out of the Shadows $10.95
Christine Jones   978-0-9827263-6-5

This is a unique book. It covers the life of Sybil Leek as experienced and shared by the author, Christine Jones, who was Sybil's friend, student, and finally in the last months of her life, her nurse.

Kindle Edition $4.99   978-0-9827263-6-5

*The Kindle version can be read on the Amazon Kindle reader or the Kindle app for iPhone

 Books of

The Crooked Path — $10.95
Selected Transcripts from the Crooked Path Podcast 978-0-9843302-0-1
Peter Paddon
Selected transcripts of the Crooked Path Podcast hosted by Peter Paddon.

The Flaming Circle — $22.95
A Reconstruction of the Old Ways of Britain and Ireland 978-0-9796168-4-6
Robin Artisson
A full working reconstruction of the pre-Christian polytheistic religious perspectives and practices of Pagan Britain and Ireland is 'taught' in the pages of this book, like a guidebook and a long letter/narrative being sent from father to children.

The Forge of Tubal Cain — $16.95
Southern California Witchcraft, Roebuck, 978-0-9796168-3-9
and the Clan of Tubal Cain
Ann Finnin
From its earliest days to the present, Ann and Dave Finnin have been at the center of the Pagan community in Southern California. Here is the story of the groups and covens that came and went, and those that grew into thriving Traditions.
Kindle Edition $4.99 978-0-9796168-3-9

The Horn of Evenwood — $27.95
Robin Artisson 978-0-9796168-0-8
The Horn of Evenwood, Also called 'The Master's Book of Conjury' or 'The Witchfather's Bloodless Bones', is a true book of Art, a Grimoire of sorcerous operations, charms, and devices of Witchery. Based on well-worn patterns and operations of Traditional sorcery and European Witchcraft from the 16th-19th centuries, this manual of magical arts provides a complete working system of Craft-sorcery.

Witchcraft

**The Kindle version can be read on the Amazon Kindle reader or the Kindle app for iPhone

Books of Witchcraft

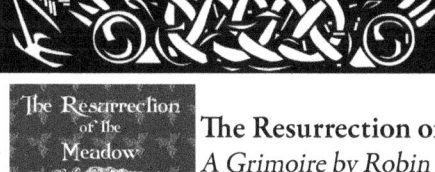

The Resurrection of the Meadow
A Grimoire by Robin Artisson

$22.95
978-0-9843302-9-4

Found within this full, self-contained working grimoire is a system of sorcery relying on the ancient spiritual aesthetic of the Faery-Faith and the Metaphysics of Elfhame- interaction with the Unseen world through the vehicle of the spirit-forms or the fetch-bodies of non-human persons that are merged with the land around us. Steeped in folklore and a much older form of deep ecology, it is a powerful work of Art for the discerning occultist.

To Fly By Night
An Anthology of Hedgewitchery
Veronica Cummer

$13.95
978-0-9827263-7-2

Hedgewitch Craft takes its name from the practice of travelling beyond the boundaries, of going past the "hedgerows" that divide what is known from what is unknown. From the ancient to the modern, from the philosophical and historical to the practical and mystical, these essays span a wide variety of paths and approaches.

Limited Edition Hardcover
Visceral Magick
Bridging the Gap Between Magic and Mundane
Peter Paddon

$45.00
Coming Soon
978-0-9843302-3-2

This book explores a set of basic experiences, ideas and techniques that used to be at the heart of every magical Tradition, but which are frequently overlooked or ignored in modern times. But they are the very things that breathe life into magical systems, the secret key that makes the magic actually work. A hardcover limited edition of Visceral Magick, including Peter Paddon's esoteric poetry and instructions on creating traditional Welsh forms of poetry. 100 signed and numbered copies

---

Witching Way of the Hollow Hill
The Gramarye of the Folk Who Dwell Below the Mound
Robin Artisson

$17.95
978-0-9820318-8-9

Author and traditional witch Robin Artisson explores these mystical themes from the perspective of The Old Faiths and pre-Christian metaphysical impulses of Europe and the British Isles. Bringing a new perspective to these ancient practices and making them more accessible, this book is a key to the door that leads into the mythical dimension of each person, and every feature of the sacred landscape.

**The Kindle version can be read on the Amazon Kindle reader or the Kindle app for iPhone

Books of

The Red Church or $24.95
The Art of Pennsylvania German Braucherei   978-0-9820318-5-8
The Traditional Blessed Healing Art for the Good of Man and Beast   548 pages
Chris Bilardi
A comprehensive guide to the history, theory and practice of Pow Wow, this book draws upon historical documentation, traditional methods, and a life of personal experience.

Special Limited Edition Hardcover $45.95   978-0-9820318-6-5
A limited edition of 100 numbered copies, including a Himmelsbrief designed by the author. This edition is only available directly from Pendraig. Copies will be signed by the author. 548 pages. ONLY A FEW COPIES LEFT!

The Raven's Flight Book of Incense, Oils, Potions and Brews $10.95
Raven Womack   978-0-9796168-1-5
Ever wonder what to do with all that crazy stuff in the metaphysical stores? Raven Womack - maker of some of the finest incenses, oils and other goodies that you will ever find - explains what they are, and how to use them.

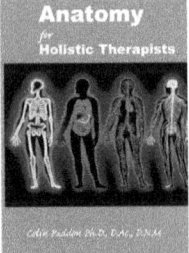

Anatomy for Holistic Therapists $10.95
Colin Paddon   978-0-9796168-2-2
Essential reading for any holistic therapist in training, this book covers the anatomy and physiology requirements for certification.

Aromatherapy For Holistic Therapists $24.95
An introduction to Aromatherapy   978-0-9820318-0-3
and its use in Holistic Therapy   500 pages, large format
Colin Paddon
Essential reading for any holistic therapist in training, this book covers all the theory requirements for certification in Aromatherapy.

Folk Magic / Herbal Holistic Therapy

**The Kindle version can be read on the Amazon Kindle reader or the Kindle app for iPhone

Books of

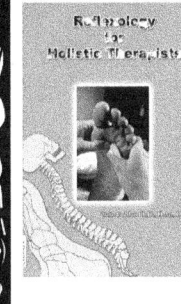

Reflexology For Holistic Therapists $12.95
Colin Paddon 978-0-9820318-2-7

Essential reading for any holistic therapist in training, this book (along with its companion DVD - sold separately) covers all the theory requirements for certification in Reflexology.

༺ ༻

All God's Creatures $10.95
Stories Old and New 978-0-9843302-6-3
Michael Berman

A collection of short stories, both traditional and contemporary, many of which can best be described as "tales of power".

༺ ༻

Journeys Outside Time $8.95
Shamanic Ballads, Shamanic Stories 978-0-9843302-7-0
Michael Berman

A collection of stories and ballads that comprise a corpus of shamanic storytelling and praxis, as told by Michael Berman, a leading expert on storytelling as a tool and as an art-form.

༺ ༻

**The Kindle version can be read on the Amazon Kindle reader or the Kindle app for iPhone

Holistic Therapy
Storytelling

Books of

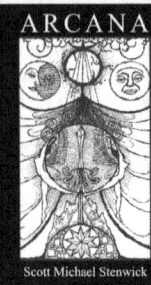

Arcana
Scott Stenwick
$17.95
978-0-9843302-5-6

Balzador was once a mighty Demon, but after opposing his master Coronzon he found himself exiled on Earth inhabiting a human body. Only one way remains for him to return home - binding together the world's magick and joining in a war against the Archons, sworn enemies of the Demons, that would upset the cosmic balance of power. Standing in his way is the Guild, a magical order founded during the European Renaissance that holds the secrets of practical magick he desperately needs to complete his task.

Golden Illuminati
Raymond Buckland
$17.95
978-0-9827263-8-9

Alec Chambers is in a quandry - his bookstore had been broken into, his storekeeper killed, and everything points to the man behind the mayhem being one of his best customers, Mr. Mathers. But when a very special journal is stolen from his own home, he finds himself in a race across Europe with Mathers and his Golden Dawn compatriots. But how are they to find the answer to the strange cypher code that is their only clue, and what is the identity of the mysterious red-haired woman?

Kindle Edition $4.99   B004GNFTOY

Son of Air and Darkness
S. P. Hendrick
$10.95
978-0-9827263-3-4

Dubhghall is a mighty warrior, trained by Scathach herself. What is more, he has been made immortal by the Morrigan, who has taught him to feast on the blood of his enemies. And because he is the grandson of Lugh, no fire nor light can harm him. But in this time of Roman rule, the Britons cry out for justice, and Dubhghall must decide whether to answer their call when he finds himself caught between the soldiers of Rome and the warriors of Boudicca.

Kindle Edition $4.99   B004F9P7QY

The Sword of the King
Vol 2 of the Glastonbury Chronicles
S. P. Hendrick
$15.95
978-0-9827263-2-7

Steven and Kevin return to fulfil their destiny once again. But right from the beginning there is trouble. Born as conjoined identical twins, it is impossible to know who is the heir to the throne, and who is to be the one who spills the sacred blood upon the ground. As if this is not enough, it seems that dark forces stir to disrupt the age-old rite, to keep them from their destiny, to deny the Land its due. Will they find its source before it is too late? And will the right blood be spilled if they do?

Kindle Edition $4.99   B004F9P7TQ

**The Kindle version can be read on the Amazon Kindle reader or the Kindle app for iPhone

Books of

The Tale of Tyrfing $8.95
Sokarjo Stormwillow 978-0-9843302-4-9

Guarded by soulless undead in the lair of a malicious dragon, a dwarven-forged sword of woe lies, waiting for the cursed son of a murdered human king. His father and brother dead at his own hands, the brutal killer will stop at nothing to claim the magical sword that will give him the power to rule the lands of Piyr in blood.

Uneasy Lies The Head $12.95
Volume 1 of the Glastonbury Chronicles 978-0-9827263-0-3
S. P. Hendrick

In the near future, Britain has given up its constitutional monarchy to become a republic. But though the crown is a museum piece and the family no longer bears its ancient titles, Stephen Windsor feels the stirrings of the lives of ancient Sacred Kings in his bones, which is not surprising as at key points in Britain's history he has been reincarnated to perform the supreme kingly act. And though the throne is empty and forgotten, the Land remembers, and calls once more for a crown upon a royal head... and royal blood upon the ground!

Kindle Edition $4.99 B004EYUIJ6

**The Kindle version can be read on the Amazon Kindle reader or the Kindle app for iPhone

---

All books and DVDs are available directly from
www.pendraigpublishing.com, Amazon's worldwide websites
and from many bookstores and metaphysical stores around the world.
For a list of international online stores that carry our products, please visit
www.pendraigpublishing.com/stores.asp

Fiction

DVDs

A Guide To Reflexology $19.95
Colin Paddon

Essential study for any holistic therapist in training, this DVD(along with its companion book, Reflexology for Holistic Therapists) covers all the theory requirements for certification in Reflexology.

Craftwise Complete Set all 5 DVDs $79.95
Peter Paddon

All five volumes of the popular Craftwise spellcrafting series by author and Witch Peter Paddon: Volume 1: Candle Magick, Volume 2: Cord Magick, Volume 3: Talismans, Volume 4: Herb Magick, Volume 5: Oils and Crystals

Craftwise Vol 1 $19.95
Candle Magick
Peter Paddon

Author and Witch Peter Paddon teaches the basics of Spellcrafting, and explores the art of Candle Magick.

Craftwise Vol 2 $19.95
Cord Magick
Peter Paddon

Author and Witch Peter Paddon teaches the basics of Spellcrafting, and explores the art of Cord Magick.

Craftwise Vol 3 $19.95
Talismans
Peter Paddon

Author and Witch Peter Paddon teaches the basics of Spellcrafting, and explores the art of Talismans.

**The Kindle version can be read on the Amazon Kindle reader or the Kindle app for iPhone

DVD's

Craftwise Vol 4 — $19.95
Herb Magick
Peter Paddon
Author and Witch Peter Paddon teaches the basics of Spellcrafting, and explores the art of herb magick.

Craftwise Vol 5 — $19.95
Oils and Crystals
Peter Paddon
Author and Witch Peter Paddon teaches the basics of Spellcrafting, and explores the art of oils and crystals.

Introduction To Faery Seership — $69.95
Orion Foxwood
The Faery Seership tradition is a collection of lore, customs, techniques, and prohibitions, which originate in the Celtic and pre-Celtic tribes of Europe. It focuses on the living inner commonwealth of the sacred land and humanity's spiritual cousins in the other world. 4 disc set.

Introduction to Southern Conjure — $19.95
with Orion Foxwood Length: 2:15
Join Orion Foxwood as he talks about the magick that surrounded him as he grew up - Southern Conjure. Learn about the history, the practice, and what makes Southern Conjure tick.

Making a Traditional Witches' Besom — $19.95
Peter Paddon
Peter Paddon - author and Witch - takes a look at the history and Lore of the besom. Then his class turns practical as he looks at the tools and materials needed to make a birch besom and demonstrates exactly how to do it.

DVD's

*The Kindle version can be read on the Amazon Kindle reader or the Kindle app for iPhone

DVD's

Making and Using Ritual Masks $19.95
Crafting Leather Masks for Trance and Journey Work
Peter Paddon

Peter Paddon, author and Witch, shares the ancient craft of constructing ritual masks from leather. Two styles are shown from start to finish, then Peter goes on to show techniques for consecrating and using the masks in circle for trance and journey work.

Orion on the Goddess $19.95
Orion Foxwood, interviewed by Katie Olivares

Children's author Katie Lydon Olivares interviews Orion Foxwood, author of "Tree of Enchantment" and "The Faery Teachings", about the Goddess. Orion answers with a depth and insight that is moving and thought-provoking.

The Sight $19.95
Getting It, Using It, Dealing With It
Peter Paddon

The Sight - the ability to see realms beyond the physical and interact with otherworldly spirits. Join Peter Paddon, author and Witch, as he explores the lore and practise of seership, and demonstrates practical exercises to develop this gift.

All books and DVDs are available directly from
www.pendraigpublishing.com, Amazon's worldwide websites
and from many bookstores and metaphysical stores around the world.
For a list of international online stores that carry our products, please visit
www.pendraigpublishing.com/stores.asp

** The Kindle version can be read on the Amazon Kindle reader or the Kindle app for iPhone

The Crooked Path

The Crooked Path Journal 1
Issue 1 Spring 2008 $9.00   978-0-9796168-8-4

Peter Paddon

Issue 1 of The Crooked Path Journal contains the following articles:
- Inside the Wicker Man - Peter Paddon
- The Origin of the Word "Witch" - R.J. Thompson
- Witch's Ritual For Getting Rid of Evil Magic - "Ku Potula" - Radomir Ristic
- Tapping the Bone - Peter Paddon
- Morning - Hedgewizard
- Usage of Animals and Animal Body Parts in Traditional Witchcraft - Radomir Ristic
- Candlemas and the Land Ceremonies Charm - R.J. Thompson
- Cosmic Soup and the Mighty Dead - Peter Paddon
- The Rite of Candlemas and the Land Ceremonies Charm - R.J. Thompson
- Blacksmith as Magus - Radomir Ristic
- Celtic Nine Poems - Peter Paddon
- As I Do Will It - Ann Finnin
- Walking the Crooked Path - Peter Paddon
- Turning The Hand of Fate - Raven Womack
- Making a Traditional Witches' Besom - Peter Paddon

Kindle Edition $1.99   0979616883

The Crooked Path Journal 2
Issue 2 Summer 2008 $9.00   978-0-9796168-9-1

Peter Paddon

Issue 2 of The Crooked Path Journal contains the following articles:
- Artemisia - Eric De Vries
- Bag of Bones - Steven Posch
- Balkan Traditional Witchcraft - Radomir Ristic
- Sympathetic Magic - R.J. Thompson
- The Call - Veronica Cummer
- The Dragon and the Dragon Slayer - Robin Artisson
- Away With the Fairies - M.V. Wragg
- Childe Ballad 243 - Steven Posch
- Scourges and Traditional Craft - Radomir Ristic
- Occult Significance of the Crossing Rite - R.J. Thompson
- Cupmarks - Steven Posch
- Great Spirits of Fate - Radomir Ristic
- Virtues and Ethics - R.J. Thompson
- Young Hornie Steals Fire - Steven Posch
- The Road Less Travelled - Peter Paddon
- Belladonna - Marilyn "Istari" R.

Kindle Edition $1.99   978-0979616891

**The Kindle version can be read on the Amazon Kindle reader or the Kindle app for iPhone

Past Issues

The Crooked Path

The Crooked Path Journal 3

Issue 3 Fall 2008

Peter Paddon

$9.00
978-0-9820318-1-0

Issue 3 of The Crooked Path Journal includes the following articles:
- The World through Eyes of Fire - Robin Artisson
- Blood Rites - Peter Paddon
- Harvest Home - R.J. Thompson
- Herbal Lore - Radomir Ristic
- If Only - Mick Wragg
- In Praise of the Lord's journey - R.J. Thompson
- Ritual Healing in Balkan Crafting - Radomir Ristic
- In Search of Gwyddbwyll - Peter Paddon
- The Mother Night's Spiral - R.J. Thompson
- Urban Witchcraft - Radomir Ristic
- Encountering Ancestors At Home and Away - Peter Paddon
- Spirits of the Hollow Hill - Eric De Vries
- Lady Fate - Kristine K
- Biblical References in Traditional Witchcraft - Peter Paddon

The Crooked Path Journal 4

Issue 4, Winter 2008/9

Peter Paddon

$9.00
978-0-9820318-4-1

Issue 4 of The Crooked Path Journal includes the following articles:
- Northern New Mexico by Grace Victoria Swann
- In search of Watto by Steven Posch
- The Black Goddess by Ann Finnin
- On the Margins by Prinny Miller
- Reconstruction and Recreation by Peter Paddon
- The Goddess Hecate (illustration) by Cherrie Button
- The Feel of Steel by Ann Finnin
- Beltaine (illustration) by Cherrie Button
- Celtic Witch (illustration) by Cherrie Button
- The Intorkatura - Sending Back by Radomir Ristic
- The Objective Astral by Ann Finnin

**The Kindle version can be read on the Amazon Kindle reader or the Kindle app for iPhone

Past Issues

The Kindle version can be read on the Amazon Kindle reader or the Kindle app for iPhone

The Crooked Path Journal 5

Issue 5, Spring 2009

Peter Paddon

$9.00
978-0-9820318-7-2

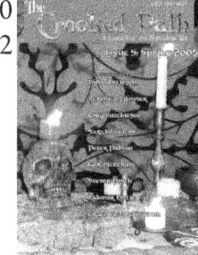

Issue 5 of The Crooked Path Journal includes the following articles:

- Moved By The Shakers by Grace Victoria Swann
- Conjure In The South by Gar Pickering
- Ancestors and Sacred Space by Peter Paddon
- Becoming a Traditional Witch by Robin Artisson
- The White Penis Cult of Forest Grove by Sarah Lawless
- Where Three Roads Meet by Cory Hutcheson
- Faerie: The Awe of the Unseen and the Unknown by Robin Artisson
- Of Faerie, Fetch and Familiar by Veronica Cummer
- Does a System of Chakras Exist in Traditional Witchcraft? by Radomir Ristic
- The Fire Brand and the Silver Thread by Robin Artisson
- Egg-Dyeing Secrets by Steve Posch
- Shaitan by Veronica Cummer
- The Origin of Coven Structure by Radomir Ristic
- Two Book Reviews by Peter Paddon

The Crooked Path Journal 6

Issue 6, Summer 2009

Peter Paddon

$9.00
978-0-9820318-9-6

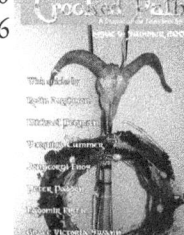

Issue 6 of The Crooked Path Journal includes the following articles:

- Beefcake, Whine and Cheese by Grace Victoria Swann
- The Drift by Jongeorgi Enos
- Shamanism by Michael Berman
- Weikerie by Robin Artisson
- To Twist and Twine by Veronica Cummer
- Witch Tales in Serbian Crafting by Radomir Ristic
- The Art of Invisibility by Peter Paddon
- The Travelling Man by Robin Artisson
- Walking Widdershins by Jongeorgi Enos

Advertising

Advertising Rates and Information

Ad Size and Rates

Two page spread	13"wide x 7.50" high	$80.00
Full Page back cover (COLOR)	7.5" wide x 9.25" high	$60.00
Full page	5.75" wide x 7.50" high	$40.00
Half Page	5.75" wide x 3.75" high	$30.00
Quarter Page	2.875 wide x 1.875" high	$20.00

There is limited spacing for two page spreads and a full page back cover (color) We can put two half size ads on the outside back cover, but *only* if there is no full page ad.

Discounts

Fifth one Free! Prepay your ad to run in four consecutive issues and receive a fifth ad of the same value free!

File Types and Format

We are able to accept most graphic file types (TIF, GIF,PDF, PNG, JPG, and DOC. etc.) with a resolution of 300 dpi or higher. Display ads must be provided as digital files (via e-mail or on CD).

Send separate files of images in case scaling down doesn't work. Alternately, text and associated graphics may be submitted, but in this case, layout of the ad will be up to the Advertising Director and Editor.

Email artwork and any other relevant materials to: ads@pendraigpublishing.com. Please include the legal and business names of the advertisers and the issue in which you would prefer your materials to appear.

*For complete details regarding
our advertising terms and conditions
please visit:
www.pendraigpublishing.com
or contact us at:
ads@pendraigpublishing.com*

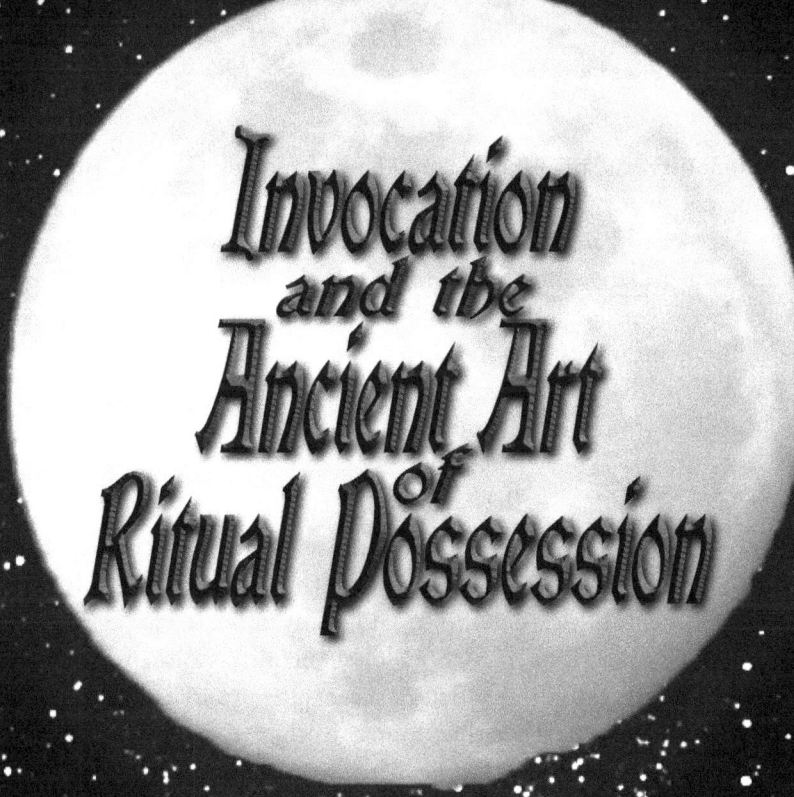

Invocation and the Ancient Art of Ritual Possession

At PantheaCon this year, I will be presenting a workshop on this subject, and I thought that as this issue of the Journal is coming out just a couple of weeks before that event, it would be very practical to write an article that compliments the workshop. The information contained here comes from many sources. Practically every teacher I have studied with has contributed in some way to what I am sharing, plus there is a lot of stuff that is the result of my own exploration and experimentation. I hope you find it useful.

What is Invocation

The Pagan community has some interesting interpretations of the word "invoke". A lot of that is due to the word being intrinsically linked to the concept of deity, and that word means different things to different people. The word "invoke" literally means "to call in ("in-voce", Latin), and is paired in most magical traditions with "evoke", which literally means "to call out", but is usually taken as meaning "to call forth". Many Pagans use the terms interchangeably, but there is a significant difference to the serious practitioner.

When we invoke, we call the deity into ourselves or another practitioner, while evocation usually involves calling the deity into a prepared space or object rather than a person. This can also be performed with other entitles, such as angelic or demonic beings, and in ceremonial magick it is the entities who are not necessarily friendly that are summoned by the act of evocation.

For the modern crafter, evocation is most often used when the presence or energy of the deity is required, but not direct interaction from them. This is the preferred practice of those who perform rites for the community, as it is gentler, easier, and less likely to freak anyone out. The big question, of course, is why we call on the deities in the first place.

Some traditions work primarily with the gods of their culture. Wicca, for example, works almost exclusively with the Goddess ("the Lady") and Her Consort, the Horned Lord. She is called on using the technique of "Drawing Down the Moon" pretty much in every rite, while the Horned Lord is called, via "Drawing Down the Sun", at appropriate times.

Those of us who work outside of Wicca often do things a little differently. If you believe, as I do, that Witchcraft is a practice rather than a religion, then you are likely to work within the religious constructs of your culture. So Italian Witches, the Stregha, work with the saints of Catholic Christianity, as do many other regional forms of witchcraft or shamanism. Wicca is a religion that openly accepts the practice of witchcraft within it, but most other religions see witchcraft as at least heretical. As a person who practices Witchcraft within a Welsh Celtic Pagan spirituality that is based on and connected to the spirituality of my ancestors, I usually call on those ancestors for "everyday" things, saving the Gods for special occasions and "the big stuff". For me, that usually means that I call on the Gods and Goddesses at the major festivals - we work the Mysteries rather than celebrate the seasons at our festivals - but rarely for spell-crafting or healing work.

Of course, the most interesting part of this for others is the techniques themselves, how we invoke our Gods. I've heard many people in the Pagan community describe magick, and spells in particular, as "prayer with props", and

I have to say that I heartily disagree with this statement. A prayer is a supplication, a cry for help, or an offering, a way of saying thank you. Spell-crafting and magick in general may make use of these as components, but they are a very different creature indeed. When you pray to a god, you are sending them a message. but when you invoke, you are calling them to come and interact, and this is a very important difference. Prayer is the tool of the worshipper, who offers up their devotion in return for the favor of their deity. Crafters don't worship their gods, so prayer becomes somewhat superfluous. What we offer our gods is respect and service. We barter with them, make deals, and explore their Mysteries and Lore in order to evolve, to become more like them. Invocation is a powerful tool in this evolutionary, experiential process, and there are several methods used by different traditions to accomplish this.

Classical Invocation

The term "invocation" is primarily used with regard to the Ceremonial Magician's technique, as more "rustic" traditions have other names for it, such as being "ridden" or "mounted". Possession has come to be associated with demonic possession, courtesy of movies like "The Exorcist", but it is a term commonly used among ethnic practitioners.

But the classical term comes with a classical technique. I like to call the classical format the three-part invocation - I don't know whether this was ever a formal way of doing it, but looking at the wording of classical "prayers" of invocation has led me to extrapolate a specific way of working based on this three-fold technique. Appropriately, there are three ways of looking at this techniques, and it is best to start with the words used.

If you look at any of the ancient invocations, you will generally see a format that consists of three parts. The words start by calling on the deity, trying to get their attention. The invocation begins by calling on the deity by one or more names, titles or epithets. Here is an example from the Golden Dawn's Invocation of the Bornless One:

> "Thee I invoke, the Bornless one.
> Thee, that didst create the Earth and the Heavens:
> Thee, that didst create the Night and the day.
> Thee, that didst create the darkness and the Light..."

In this case, the titles, etc., are replaced by a list of the deity's achievements. The celebrant then moves to the second phase, where they speak directly to the deity as present before them, often citing their authority for calling on them:

> "I am_____ Thy Prophet, unto Whom Thou didst commit Thy Mysteries, the Ceremonies of_____:
> Thou didst produce the moist and the dry, and that which nourisheth all created Life.
> Hear Thou Me, for I am the Angel of Apophrasz Osorronophris: this is Thy True Name, handed down to the Prophets of_____..."

Finally, the celebrant speaks as the deity, signifying that the invocation is complete and successful:

"I am He! the Bornless Spirit! having sight in the Feet: Strong, and the Immortal Fire!
I am He! the Truth!
I am He! Who hate that evil should be wrought in the World!
I am He, that lightningeth and thundereth.
I am He, from whom is the Shower of the Life of Earth:
I am He, whose mouth flameth:
I am He, the Begetter and Manifester unto the Light:
I am He, the Grace of the World:
"The Heart Girt with a Serpent" is My Name!"

In a ritual where the deity is being called to share words of wisdom, it is common for the last words of the invocation to be the words of the deity, as the hardest part of the process after opening yourself up is letting the deity use your mouth. But we'll talk about that later.

The key to all this verbiage is that, besides its sheer commonsense (get their attention, invite them in, listen to what they say), it allows for an interplay of energy to take place. Invocations that involve a formal spoken component are nearly always conducted by a group rather than a solitary individual. The natural rhythm of the piece allows an interplay of energy to occur, where the celebrant, standing in the center or at the focal point of the rite, intones the first part of the invocation, extending energy towards the participants in order to "light the fire". The participants then intone the second section, taking the energy from the celebrant and amplifying it by each participant returning the full amount of the energy to the celebrant. This amplified energy is then used by the celebrant to raise their vibration to the point where the deity can sep in, by using the visualization described below, or a variant of it. The final step is when the celebrant, now inhabited by the deity, speaks the words of the deity and encompasses the other participants in the energy brought in with the deity, thus raising their energies so that they two can perceive and interact with their God.

The visualization is the key to this type of invocation, and the one I give here is not specific to any particular magical lodge or group, but is rather a generic one I have formulated for teaching purposes.

The celebrant begins by visualizing themselves as starting to grow larger as they begin the invocation. With every word, they grow larger and larger, until by the end of the first section, they see themselves as being so large that planet earth is a footstool, on which they are standing. From this expanded vantage point, they look out from the center of a huge circle comprising every deity of their pantheon, and as the words of the participants, and their amplified energy, lifts them up, the visualization becomes something more, and the deity they are calling steps towards them, and then takes up a position immediately behind the. The full impact of the amplified energy raises their vibration to a point where the deity is able to step forward into them, inhabiting their body, and the celebrant/deity then visualizes shrinking back down to normal size, the celebrant bringing the deity down into the Temple within themselves. The deity then speaks the final words of the invocation, and then begins to converse and interact with the participants in order to achieve the goal of the rite.

This technique can be used by a solitary practitioner, but it is somewhat pointless to do so, as you are effectively inviting the deity into a room to converse, and having nobody there to talk to them once they arrive. However, there are three levels of invocation that don't often get talked about in ceremonial circles, though they are more familiar to the practitioners of shamanic or folk magick traditions. These three levels are usually referred to as aspect, contact and possession.

An aspect of a deity is where you draw the energy or potency of the deity into the ritual space, but not the personality or "presence" of the deity themselves. This is a useful tool for augmenting healing, charging tools, amulets or talismans, or bringing in extra energy for some other purpose. In this case, instead of the deity stepping into the celebrant in the above visualization, they merely connect energetically with the celebrant, who then brings down the power as if they were bringing in an extension cord from another room.

A contact with a deity is often described as being like a phone call from the deity - the celebrant can "hear" them and speak with them, but the other participants cannot, so the celebrant relays messages to and fro. This requires less effort and skill to maintain, so it can be a very viable way to work with a group that is new and not used to working together yet.

A possession by a deity is exactly what it sounds like... the deity temporarily takes full control of the celebrant's body and uses it to interact with the other participants.

Contact and Possession

For witches and other crafters, there is a much simpler way of working with contacts and possessions, one that does not require the formality and verbiage of the ceremonial approach. Crafters tend to work their magick from the opposite direction of ceremonialists. Whereas ceremonial magicians place themselves at the center of the universe and draw everything into themselves, crafters tend to go out "between the worlds", and encounter gods and heroes in their own realms. This is also achieved through visualization, but it is a much more natural and easy set of images. The celebrant simply goes into trance state through any one of countless techniques, themselves themselves in a location that is significant to the deity. The god or goddess shows up, and the celebrant regulates whether this is a contact or possession by controlling how close they are to the deity in the visualization. The important part of this technique is being able to open the gateway at the base f the skull, the traditional entry point for spirits, gods and ancestors.

It is a good idea, especially if you are new to this, or you are calling in a deity you are not truly familiar with, to set guards at the gateway. traditionally a crafter will set their Matron and Patron as gatekeepers, but if you don't have those, you can call on a spirit guide or ancestor, and their task is to make sure that the only entity or entities who enters that gateway are the ones who are supposed to be there.

Once the visualization of the location is established, the celebrant calls on the deity - this need only be done internally - and when they respond, you will find that as you move closer, you begin to feel a merging taking place, and you will find a point a few feet from the deity where your sense of self is completely overwhelmed, but when you move back away from them, you feel your sense of self to retain.

This moving closer and further away is the mechanism for consciously controlling whether you are contacting or possessing, but you will find that there is a natural ebb and flow of the experience, so you will actually experience a range from strong contact to strong possession during the course of the rite.

Shamanic Possession - Being "Mounted"

Many indigenous shamanic practitioners make use of the technique of being "ridden" or "mounted" by their gods. This is a well-known part of Santeria, Voudoun and Ifa religions. It essentially involves going into trance and using the rhythm of drum and/or chant to draw a spirit, ancestor or deity into the celebrant. Many of the tribal cultures allow for this to happen spontaneously in the "congregation", and it is how they pick the ones with aptitude to train further in their Mysteries. Interestingly, the same process can be seen in some of the charismatic denominations of Christianity, such as the ones who speak in tongues, the shakers and snake-handlers.

For the modern western practitioner of Old craft Ways, this can be an effective technique for those already fairly experienced in the other methods. I like to call it the "quickening", after the events in the movie "Highlander", because I found that the scene where McCleod runs on the beach with the stag was a major inspiration for me in developing my own version of this way of interacting with the gods.

Getting into a trance state can be done effectively using a number of techniques, the easiest being the use of drums, dance and chant, but once the celebrant is in a trance, it can be quickly deepened and transformed into a mounting by using this simple technique. Two other participants take up a position close to the celebrant, one right behind each shoulder. Alternating from one side to the other, and using a regular heart-beat rhythm to start with, they begin to alternately whisper the name of the deity. Gradually, they increase the speed and intensity of the whisper, until it becomes obvious that the celebrant has become possessed by that deity.

It is important to bear in mind the nature of the visualization that the celebrant uses during this - they should be visualizing the deity in an appropriate setting, coming ever closer until the possession occurs. However, the nature of the image used will define the nature of the possession. A prime example of this was the first time my coven, Briar Rose, tried this technique. We had chosen to call on Herne, and the celebrant for this occasion visualized Herne as a majestic stag on the moor. You can imagine our reaction when the possession took hold - and it really does "take" very suddenly with this technique - and we found ourselves in the powerful presence of what felt like a fully grown stag in his prime, ready to fight, rut or run. We could even smell his musk, and the presence was very physical, very "weighted". Of course, Herne in this form was not interested in conversing, so we released him and brought the celebrant out of his trance state.

A while later, we tried again, but we were careful to make sure that the celebrant visualized Herne as the Hunter...

Conclusion

So what are the hallmarks of a successful invocation? Well, that depends on what you are aiming for. Participants should be aware of a certain energy about the celebrant while the deity is present - obviously this will vary depending upon the ability of the participant, but they should at least notice there is something different. If the deity is present and interacting, it will show in the eyes, a sort of intensity and otherworldliness that is hard to fake. There are also likely to be subtle differences in mannerisms and posture.

The more shamanic, visceral forms of possession, however, tend to be a lot more obvious. The eyes are much stronger in their intensity than the celebrant's usual gaze, and there is often a curious fluidity to the movements of the body that is hard to describe, but impossible to miss once experienced. he energy and intensity with possessions is much les subtle than with invocations.

Unfortunately, there are some who will fake a possession in order to pursue an agenda or to attract attention to themselves, but with a little experience, they are easy to spot. Primarily, the absence of the energy and intensity are a big giveaway, but even a complete novice can watch out for certain signs. To start with, many who fake a possession do so in order to castigate or demean another participant. I can't say this for certain for all cultures, but certainly with the western pantheons I have never observed a deity putting down someone in public, during a group ritual. The gods always seem to manage to do that in private. Also, deities seem to be very aware of peoples personal space - I have never seen a deity grope a participant unless there is already an established relationship with them that involves intimacy as a spiritual or magical process, so if the celebrant is touching people inappropriately it is highly likely to be a fake possession. But once you have developed enough ability to sense energy, you will never mistake a fake possession for the real thing.

Incidentally, there is one interesting thing about possessions that I have noticed, that appears to have no rhyme or reason, but seems to be fairly universal... if the possession is done standing, the deity will have free rein to move about the sacred space, interacting physically with the participants. But if the celebrant is seated for the possession, while the deity might wave their arms and gesticulate, they will remain seated, and interact only verbally with the participants.

The experience for the celebrant is often profound, though it may be initially confusing. Traditionally it is said that the celebrant will remember nothing of a full possession, but because possession occurs with an ebb and flow of intensity, the end result is that the celebrant often remembers thing in a one-person-removed way. I've heard people describe it has the words coming from their own mouths sound like the "waa-waa-waa" sound that adults make in the Peanuts cartoons, and others who experience it the way I do, as if the deity and I are over in a corner having our own conversation, and I hear the words spoken to the other participants by the deity (using my physical mouth) as a conversation across the room that I catch snippets of.

The benefits for the celebrant are on several levels. Firstly, as an act of service to the group, it is a powerful way of expressing your commitment to the Path, but there is a very real benefit in that possession s a visceral experience, and regular practice of possession facilitates an increase and evolution of the ability to manifest magick in all areas of life, making all magical acts more powerful and profound.

Peter Paddon is an author, podcaster, and Magister of Briar Rose, a small coven of modern cunningfolk. You can experience him discussing and demonstrating the magick of ritual possession in his workshop at PantheaCon, the largest Pagan event on the West Coast, held on President's Day weekend in San Jose, CA.

GARDNER REDUX

by Ann Finnin

The Crooked Path Journal

At the Day for Gerald, a conference held in London on Sept 12, 2010, I finally met a man I never really knew before.

Gerald Brousseau Gardner

Oh, I had heard about him for a long time. For the last forty years, the stories about Gerald Gardner, founder of Modern Wicca, abounded, especially here in the States, where he had taken on an almost mythic status. He even has self-appointed descendents and apostles who consider him something of a Pagan Prophet, a man whose writings, rituals and pronouncements must not be questioned and must be followed to the letter – even when the letter is proven to be wrong.

But to most everyone else, he was at best a talented ritualist and researcher who was able to revive an ancient form of goddess worship which had languished underground for two millenia. At worst, he was a sexual pervert who did nothing but come up with a quasi-religious framework for what was little more than a bondage fetish.

The truth proved to be more complex, and a lot more compelling.

Through the period photos presented by Gardner biographer Phil Heselton, we met Gardner as the asthmatic younger son of a wealthy lumber merchant who was exiled to the 'warmer climates' of Ceylon and Malaysia in the care of an irresponsible nanny. Despite the social class of his birth, Gardner grew up apart from his British peers and learned little to nothing of the behavior expected of him. He was even forced to teach himself to read and became essentially self-taught with the enviable advantage of being able to study what he wanted when he wanted without any of the superfluous impedimenta of what was a 'proper' British public school education.

But perhaps the most poignant and significant thing I learned about his early life involved his relationship with the natives of the countries he lived and worked in for most of his life. Unlike his social peers, he never seemed to consider the natives as inferiors to be exploited and abused, but more like friends and neighbors to be treated as equals. So, he managed to earn their trust to the extent that he was invited to attend some of their secret ceremonies and rituals. This early exposure to genuine folk magic had a profound influence on his later work.

Later, when he returned to England, Gardner made the rounds of the occult scene that was prevalent at the time. He became a nudist. He joined the Co-Masons. He participated in the highly theatrical rituals of a local Rosicrucian lodge. It was there that he met the mysterious 'Old Dorothy' Clutterbuck who initiated him into something he later called 'Wica,' a cult which, according to author Margaret Murray, had been prevalent among the English upper classes (the sort of people who joined the Order of the Garter) since at least the twelfth century.

It was a nice story, but it seems to be just that – a story.

We still have no idea who 'Old Dorothy' really was or if the New Forest Coven that initiated Gardner had any connection to the 'witch' cult described by Murray. There doesn't seem to be anything in Gardner's rituals, or in his past associations that indicate it. All of the material in his writings can be easily traced to published sources – much of it since discredited. And most of the claims that either he or his initiates made to being from witch families have been found to be fabrication.

So, did Gardner actually receive an initiation in the New Forest that provides him and his descendents with an unbroken lineage of spiritual authority that dates back to the Middle Ages?

In short, no.

Does it matter?

No.

Gardner seems to have learned as much about traditional witchcraft from the natives in Malaya, Ceylon and Borneo than he ever did from Dorothy Clutterbuck at the New Forest. From her, her colleagues in Co-masonry and the Rosicrucian lodges and from Crowley and the OTO, he learned the art of writing rituals employing the symbolism of the Western Esoteric Tradition. But rituals do not a religion make. Something else, something undocumented, un-provable but extremely powerful became infused into Gardner's rituals. And that was what made Wica (or Wicca) what it eventually became.

Thanks to the historian Ron Hutton, we were also able to see Gardner as a man who was something of a stranger in his own land. He exhibited an almost childlike naivety; never really learning the often hypocritical social manners of his station. He took people at face value, which often resulted in betrayal, it never occurring to him that his associates would have motivations other than the dedication and devotion that he had. He was past middle age by the time he began his work. He didn't have much time left, and didn't want to waste what time he had on what he considered to be other people's petty personal issues.

What about all the lurid stories of inviting reporters to attend rituals? The best reason for this seems to be that Gardner was an evangelist of a sort. He wanted to bring his revelation of the Goddess to the public's attention in case anyone who was interested in this sort of spiritual quest could know what he was up to. This attitude, coupled with his indifference to what society in general thought of him led him to seek publicity – not for himself necessarily but for his new religion. That others didn't share either his zeal or his immunity to social ostracism wasn't important. Hence, the resentment of those he worked with.

And what was up with all the binding and whipping?

As traditional Gardnarians have pointed out for a number of years, binding and flagellation was an ancient form of trance induction that is practiced all over the world. Pain can result in an altered state of consciousness, as anybody who has endured a Native American Sundance can tell you. Inflicting pain in measured doses to induce trance was an integral part of the native rituals that Gardner likely witnessed. He knew that he wouldn't be able to duplicate these methods in a more 'civilized' society, so he introduced a method that would hopefully do the job without the risk. The binding and scourging Gardner practiced was not intended to be painful. It is not equivalent to beating someone's bottom bloody with birch twigs, as was done to young men in Victorian times. The swats should certainly be felt, and might even sting, but they should not be so hard as to raise welts. This was not their purpose.

We have to realize that at this point in time, Gardner was an old man in bad health. Binding of the wrists and throat to restrict blood flow to the brain and rhythmic stimulation at the base of the spine was probably one of the few methods of trance induction that he could engage in. Other methods, such as dancing around in a circle until exhaustion and hyperventilation sets in, were probably out of the question.

Was he sexually aroused by it? Probably. Anybody who has done any kind of magic knows full well that the energy used in magical ritual often begins as sexual arousal before it is sublimated by various means to other purposes. However, as Hutton pointed out, nowhere in any of Gardner's papers and effects can one find any depiction of what might be considered today as B&D porn. So, if he was indeed aroused by this method, that arousal was more a means to an end than as an end in itself – in other words, he used his aroused energy for magical purposes not for sexual gratification.

We also saw Gardner through the eyes of those who worked with him. Lois Bourne, Fred Lamond, Philip Carr-Gomm and Zachary Cox all described Gerald as a visionary, gentle and likeable with a good sense of humor, something of a trickster but a man who had somehow gotten a hold of something ancient and powerful that even he didn't fully understand and was determined to bring to the world anyway by any means possible. Whatever else he was, Gardner truly believed in what he was doing and that made an indelible impression on even those people who considered him a fraud.

Another significant thing about Gardner and his new pagan religion that Hutton pointed out was that he and his early followers came from a particular social and economic class that had arisen in Britain (and in most of Western Europe and America) as a result of the Industrial Revolution. They were not members of the traditional aristocracy, whose scions and fortunes had been decimated in the trenches of World War I, but they were not working class tradesmen either. Neither were they from the vanishing remnants of the peasantry who still worked the land as their forefathers had for centuries.

Instead, they were the bourgeoisie, the sons and daughters of wealthy merchants and professional people who generally had three advantages that made occult work and participation in magical groups in general possible -- advantages that the working classes didn't have. They had money enough to not have to work long hours to make a living, they had leisure time to read books and attend rituals, meetings and lectures, and they had the advantage of a classical education which included the history and mythology of Greece, Rome and Egypt. So, neopagan occultism, of the sort practiced by Gardner as well as Crowley, Mathers and others, was an upper middle class phenomenon where people could afford to be eccentric.

Gardner, however, didn't seem to exploit this advantage, as did many of his Victorian contemporaries. In general, he lived a sane and sober early life without indulging in the debauchery that has become so notorious in accounts of turn-of-the-century occultists. Even though he liked opium, he didn't seem to have the drug addiction problems that plagued Crowley. He seems to have lived within his means, paid his creditors on time, remained faithful to his wife and kept himself out of jail. Yes, he was flamboyant, notorious and eccentric in his later years and the newspapers loved to be shocked by him. And yet, he did no one, least of all himself, any harm. More than anything, his life proved that one doesn't have to engage in self-destructive behavior in order to be an occultist.

Finally, we heard from a panel consisting of Morgana, Julia Philips, Vivian Crowley, Rufus Harrington, Prudence Jones and Zach Cox – all of who had been active in Gardnarian craft for decades and who were concerned with outreach to the larger pagan community. If Wicca was to avoid remaining nothing more than an exclusive private club for upper middle class dilettantes, it had to find a way to meet the religious needs of people in the greater society. How would Wiccans marry? How would they be buried? What would they do about wills and family responsibilities?

In America, Wiccan groups can avoid some of these legal issues by incorporating as a church. In England, this isn't possible since the Anglican church is considered part of the government. In Europe, the term 'church' has different connotation, less authoritarian and more concerned with community identity. But in all cases, the term carries with it certain emotional baggage that is best avoided. So how, then, does Wicca avoid threats to its existence, or at least to the open practice of it.

One threat that was mentioned was fundamentalism and I was pleased that at least one panel member had the courage to include pagan fundamentalism in that threat. Wiccans are just as prone to excoriate each other for heresy as Christians are. Still, the Christian society in which we live can make things extremely difficult for Wiccans to practice their faith openly. Wiccans must learn to take advantage of existing laws against religious harassment that were designed to protect them.

Some laws that might prove to be a threat have nothing to do with religious freedom. Britain's health and safety regulations might make some aspects of Wicca practice, such as herbal healing, illegal. Still, all the panelists cautioned us against being overly paranoid. Wicca has many friends in the greater society, with more being made all the time. It is part of a broader evolution of consciousness, one in which Gardner made a significant contribution. In only forty years, his religion had gone global. The fact that pagans from Britain, America, Europe and Australia had all come together to honor him bears a testament to that contribution. He has planted seeds that it is up to us to nurture.

It may take a hundred years for the seeds that Gardner planted to flower. And what we may see in a hundred, two hundred or five hundred years may be unrecognizable from what we see today. Perhaps some religious historian in 2500 will publish a study on the history of Wicca in the twentieth century and will quote Heselton and Hutton as ancient and irrefutable sources.

I'll look forward to reading it in my next incarnation.

Ann Finnin (Tujunga, California) holds degrees in biology and experimental psychology and works as a technical writer for a biotech company. Her books include 'The Forge of Tubal Cain' and 'The Sorcerer of Sainte Felice'. Ann and her husband Dave live with their big black Lab, Hunter.

The Crooked Path
A Journal of the Nameless Art

Book of the Season Spotlight

In each issue The Crooked Path will give readers a special sneak peek inside one of the wonderful books published through Pendraig Publishing.

The Winter Spotlight shines on

Visceral Magick by Peter Paddon

Nightmares of Lilith

Despite the name, this actually has very little to do with Lilith, other than the fact that she is the "Bringer of Nightmares". It is also a visceral experience that cannot be consciously triggered, but instead seems to be a spontaneous part of the opening up of the visceral intelligence. You can't plan for it, but there is a good chance that you will experience it at some point in your spiritual journey.

Most people are caught unaware by this experience. Even those who have heard of it and know details about it tend to find its appearance to be a complete surprise. The Nightmares tend to take the form of bloody nightmares that frequently involve either more gore than you could usually handle, or distressing events that have the same overall effect. My own experience, for example, involved a lot of blood and internal organs, but I have heard of other accounts where the dreamer spent several nights killing kittens in various ways – she was a cat lover, so this was as distressing to her as my own organ-spewing dreams.

These dreams tend to continue over a course of about a week, ending only when the dreamer either surrenders to the experience or rejects it completely. They tend to have little or no clues to their esoteric nature, until you reach the end of the series, when they invariably end with a profound encounter with the Black Goddess, or a cultural equivalent.

In my case, the dreams began with a fairly standard – for me – nightmare. I should point out that I am a little strange (in case you hadn't already guessed), and I actually enjoy nightmares because I see them as my own personal horror movies. This one was a little different, though, because my nightmares are not normally gory, and it became more and more bloody as the dream progressed. It took place in a railway yard... lots of tracks, engines, rolling stock – mostly freight containers, though there were some passenger carriages. I was with someone I didn't recognize, who was being pursued, and for most of the dream we never saw the pursuers, but went from near-escape to near-escape in classic horror-movie style, seeing a shadow or feeling/hearing a presence without actually seeing directly what was after us.

Of course, the time came when the pursuers – zombies – broke through and ripped my anonymous companion to shreds, and then the dream became more frantic. In the end I was cornered, but I ;literally tore two of the zombies apart with my hands to make my escape, and the dream ended.

The next night involved a road-trip of some sort, with my fellow coveners on board. We were going from town to town searching for something, and one by one the others on the bus were taken out, until there were only myself and one other left. At this point we found the entrance to a cave system, and on entering the caves, we found an ancient temple at the far side of a labyrinth, where some of our missing companions were trying to reconstruct the ancient ritual that used to be performed there. They had robes and regalia that were apparently copies of the originals, but were having little success. This resulted in large bat-like creatures carrying them off, one by one, until only the Mistress of the coven was left. By this time, I had found a side cave, where the original robes and regalia were hidden, and the three of us were able to complete the ritual and banish the bat-like creatures, though not without the unnamed companion being torn to shreds by the creatures.

The next few nights involved me travelling from place to place in a car, on foot, and finally on a motorbike. The towns I encountered were practically uninhabited, post-apocalyptic, but each night there were a handful of people, often being hunted by a psychopath or creature of some sort.

The final night was different, though. I was riding my motorbike in torrential rain, and arrived in the center of a one-horse town that appeared deserted. Standing before a billboard that I could not read in an abandoned bus station, I suddenly realized where I needed to be (without consciously knowing where that was). I mounted the bike, turned around and headed out of town through the rain. It was late, around midnight.

After battling the bike through the wet weather for what seemed like an eternity, I found myself outside a run-down house filled with bikers partying. I went inside, to find that as I entered the room it went silent – not in the "stranger enters the bar" way, but a respectful silence as everyone acknowledged me. As I went through to the next room, the people there fell into the same respectful silence, while the room I left erupted into the life and noise of the party once again. Room after room I encountered the same, until I finally came upon a room that was empty except for what appeared to be a huge, oversized motorbike. The door behind me closed, and I realized that there was somebody reclining on the bike, a huge "Venus of Willendorf" proportioned female whose age I could not discern. She was naked, covered in deep black tribal tattoos, though her skin was white, and the tattoos were moving. She was, of course, the Black Mother, and I climbed up onto the motorbike and was embraced by her – this was at once a sexual and non-sexual encounter, resulting in the tattoos that covered her also covering me.

The key to all of this was that each nightmare came to a satisfactory conclusion once I surrendered to it. When I overcame my revulsion and did what was necessary, I was able to move forward. Finally, I met the Black Goddess, and knowing I was going to my doom, I embraced her and everything she represents.

Since that final night, I have encountered Her in my dreams, but She does not waste Her time with the gore any more. Instead she gives me dreams that inspire my waking rituals, and my writing. Although the Nightmares of Lilith are a powerful visceral tool for developing your abilities, they are above all a sign that you are on the right track. On the flip-side, they are a challenge that tests your ability to surrender to the bloody events you encounter, to do what is necessary. I believe there are parallels with eastern exercises, such as the Buddhist "contemplating the self as a rotting corpse".

One important thing to note is that the Nightmares of Lilith are not pleasant – they deliberately target your boundaries by making use of imagery and actions that repulse you personally. For this reason most people reject them when they occur, and they go away. I do not know for sure if, once rejected, they will ever return, but I believe that they will cycle round again after a time, when you other efforts at spiritual evolution bring you to another place that is conducive to invoking them.

The key to completing this experience is truly to surrender yourself to the experience. This is not only traumatic at the time, but it will have knock-on effects. Some of these are going to be the mental and spiritual aspects of coping with the experience, but the plus side is that there are few experiences that will bring your visceral magick into manifestation better than the Nightmares. Once they have been experienced, it is as if the connection between the "rational" mind and the visceral intellect are hard-wired, allowing a huge leap in ability to be made. This increase in ability can be made without the Nightmares, but they really do act as a kind of short-cut.

Peter Paddon is an author and witch, the Magister of Briar Rose, a small coven of cunningfolk. He is a Brit of Welsh ancestry who lives in Los Angeles with his wife Linda. His books include, 'A Grimoire for Modern Cunning Folk' and 'The Crooked Path: Selected Transcripts'

This is an excerpt from "Visceral Magick", which is about to be published by Pendraig Publishing, and will be launched at the 2011 PantheaCon in San Jose, CA.

The Crooked Path Journal

Before the Battle

There is a tension in my shoulders
Fear and excitement combined within
To start adrenaline flowing
As we begin to dress

My armor, such as it is
I strap on now in earnest
Checking every piece, everything
Not this time for practice
But to take my place
Serving my household
And my people's cause.

We marched across the footbridge
Onto the battlefield
My eyes wide, taking in both friend and foe.
I resist the urge to flee,
And wait for call to charge.
Apprehension fills my soul – can I do this thing?
Do I have a Warriors heart?
Or shall I leave the field
scarred in mind and soul, ashamed?

At last the call is called:
Two armies now advance
A warriors cry springs from my lips
At last I live, I live!

by Peter Paddon

www.ingramcontent.com/pod-product-compliance
Lightning Source LLC
Chambersburg PA
CBHW081501040426
42446CB00016B/3342